The Project Management Workbook

The Project Management Workbook

Field-Proven Strategies for
Managing Your Greatest Asset

Nancy B. Cobb

McGraw-Hill

New York   Chicago   San Francisco   Lisbon
London   Madrid   Mexico City   Milan   New Delhi
San Juan   Seoul   Singapore   Sydney   Toronto

The *McGraw-Hill* Companies

1   2   3   4   5   6   7   8   9   0   AGM/AGM   0   9   8   7   6   5   4   3   2

ISBN 0-07-140840-1

McGraw-Hill books are available at special quantity discounts to use as premiums and sales promotions, or for use in corporate training sessions. For more information, please write to the Director of Special Sales, Professional Publishing, McGraw-Hill, Two Penn Plaza, New York, NY 10121-2298. Or contact your local bookstore.

 This book is printed on recycled, acid-free paper containing a minimum of 50% recycled, de-inked fiber.

Library of Congress Cataloging-in-Publication Data

Cobb, Nancy B.
    The project management workbook : field-proven strategies for managing your greatest asset by Nancy B. Cobb.
        p.   cm.
ISBN 0-07-140840-1 (pbk. : alk. paper)
1. Project management. 2. Teams in the workplace. 3. Organizational effectiveness. I. Title
    HD69.P75 C617   2002
    658.4′04—dc21

                                                    2002011424

Contents

Preface

A consultant's job, according to my philosophy, is to provide the client with the tools and support needed to become more independent, to be a subject-matter expert and coach, and to be a knowledge and emotional intelligence provider. That's how this book began.

During my corporate life, I was always teaching others how to integrate social and technical changes, especially during projects. That was my job, and I loved it because each project offered new challenges to my internal clients and to me. Then, when I started consulting, I found myself doing the same thing—teaching others how to work effectively with the people side of projects. I was surprised that this was such a new and undeveloped concept to others. People knew that they needed help on the people side of things; they just didn't know how to get it and few had the internal expertise. Of course, it may sound too touchy-feely for technical people to bother with. They didn't incorporate this "people side" into the project process formally because they couldn't measure it easily, and people are messy (they have many issues to consider); yet informally, they knew that it was the cause of over 50 percent of their project problems. The reality is that it *is* a business issue; it *must* be a part of the project management process; and it *can* be measured, as I demonstrate with my initial case study ("Show Me the Money," Chapter 1).

So as I started developing a few tools for my clients, I realized that it was time to write my experiences and recommendations down more formally so that they would have a resource to work with when they were on their own. Never was it my intention to write a book—just some helpful worksheets and ideas. When someone asked if I planned to publish it because there just wasn't anything practical out there, I realized that there was a need that I could fill and thus, the birth of *The Project Management Workbook*.

DOING SOME RESEARCH—THE SURVEY

Before making that final decision, I decided to do some research and see what other people who have worked on projects thought, as well as what other books were in the marketplace. Starting off with a survey on some Web sites, I was led to some very immediate and meaty feedback. Within 24 hours there were over 50 responses, and within another few hours, 15 completed surveys. These completed surveys weren't of the "yes" and "no" variety of answers, but were passionate responses about their frustrating "people" project experiences. Some wrote two and three pages about how important the people issues were on projects, and how uneducated people were in dealing with them. What an eye opener!

The survey asked five basic questions ranging from "Did you ever receive any formal training on the people side of project management?" to "What people issues have you experienced?" Much to my surprise, of those who completed the survey, only four had received any formal training in school, but what they were taught came in the "risk management" portion of a class or was anecdotal in nature. Only one of the survey participants had a Team Dynamics class (an elective). A few had taken a workshop or had gone to a seminar once they were in the field.

On the other side of the questions, it was unanimous that they all felt the people side was critical, and in fact, would make or break a project. Having to learn the hard way—by trial and error—had left many respondents more than eager for information and ideas. Their support for my book was overwhelming! Although this wasn't a statistically validated process, their answers and my experience were enough to reinforce my assumption that there was a need for more information.

DOING SOME RESEARCH—EDUCATION TODAY

With that encouragement, I decided that I also needed to explore what was happening *now* in the world of higher education, as it relates to the people side of project management. So off I went to major universities in the Midwest that offered engineering programs. I contacted many department heads, explained what I was doing, and asked if they had any courses available to their students about the people side of project management. The first two laughed at me and said "We don't do that," another said, "I think we have an Organizational Behavior class, but it's an elective," while another said that they relied on the supporting MBA courses. Unfortunately, it appeared that not much had changed. "Techies" still just concentrate on technology! It was suggested that I teach a workshop or class for them, which was encouraging. At last look, the Organizational Behavior class that was offered was oversubscribed to— that's promising! It should be said that this was just a midwestern observation but it was enough to make me realize that not enough was being taught, because these were well-respected universities.

DOING SOME RESEARCH—OTHER BOOKS

My last bit of encouragement came from exploring the world of books. Again, off to the Internet. My stomach sank when I found that there were 1187 books on project management. My first thought was, "Just what the world needs, another project management book!" I took a few days to go through the long list. I found that about 35 percent were about how to use Microsoft Project, another 40 percent were on the technical process of project management, and about 20 percent were on specialized project management (e.g., project management in third-world countries). Bottom line, I could only find about 20 books that seemed to focus just on people and projects. As I then hunted those books down, I found that many did a great job describing behavioral theory. However, I couldn't find anything quite as simple and practical as what I had in mind for my book.

GO FOR IT!

With those findings, off I was to write and publish a simple, easy-to-use book about people on projects. It didn't really matter to me if a reader devoured the whole book; it was more important that they found what they needed, and that it helped support their business goals in a practical way! I wasn't out to explain behavioral theory, but I was out to illustrate everyday, realistic ideas that are based on behavioral theory.

What I hoped would be no more than 100 pages grew, once I realized just how much there was to say and how many examples there were to give. I still feel that I've just touched the tip of the iceberg, and I realize that this may be just a starting point for many people using it.

Dedication and Acknowledgments

Thanks to all my coworkers at Nabisco, especially the Chicago Bakery, who partnered with me while learning and growing through the many project management experiences that provided the substance of this book. Special thanks goes to the best cheerleader and subject matter expert, Dan Pettit, who was with me from beginning to end on this project, always offering words of encouragement as well as his technical perspective. Thanks to John Healy and Al Edwards who, as clients, ignited my interest as well as reinforced the need for a practical book like this. John continually had words of support and enthusiasm to offer, which were dearly appreciated. Bret Nicholaus and Barbara A. Glanz, authors themselves, willingly gave their insight and feedback on literary questions, which made me realize that publishing this was possible. And most importantly, my appreciation goes to special friends, Penny Davoren and Erin Higby Page, who advised me with editing recommendations, as well Kathleen Massat and Andy Metropole, who offered their expert technical insight and recommendations. Appreciation also goes to the many people who participated in my research survey—your response made it clear how important and unattended to the people side of project management is, giving me my final reason for writing this. Lastly, thanks goes to McGraw-Hill for allowing me to share my ideas through this published book, and especially my editor, Ela Aktay, who patiently walked me through each step of the process.

I dedicate this book to all those out there who are looking for practical advice and sample formats that will make their projects more successful.

I also dedicate it to my late mother, Ethel Carraro, whose passion was writing, and my dear granddaughter, Sydney, whose eyes hold the future of all that is possible.

My last dedication goes out in memory of my Dad, Gil Carraro, who asked that I give him the first copy of my book. Unfortunately, he died a month before it came out, so although I won't be able to keep my promise, I want to acknowledge the fond memories I have of him and the support he always provided.

The Project Management Workbook

1

What's It All About?

This user-friendly guide is for all of those who may be a part of a project team or affected by what the project team is doing. It is also for those in school learning how to complete projects successfully through effective project management.

Most certainly, it's for:

- Engineering
  - Project Managers
  - Project Engineers
  - Disciplined Design Engineers
  - Plant Engineers
  - Engineering and Operations Students
- Operations
  - Production Managers
  - Supervisors
  - Maintenance Staff
  - Sanitation
- Purchasing
- Quality
- Safety

- Human Resources
  - Employee Relations
  - Training and Development
  - Trainers
- Vendors
- Contractors

WHAT IS THE PROJECT MANAGEMENT WORKBOOK?

The Project Management Workbook refers to all the aspects of a project that will be needed to *support* the technology—the nontechnical components. In most cases, this means people, in particular the end users and what they need to make the project succeed. These people include the operators, maintenance staff, vendors, operations personnel, human resources staff, and everyone else associated with the project. Yes, that probably means you too!

Have you ever heard project engineers, in their most frustrating moments, say, "if it weren't for the people, we'd have this thing up and running in no time." Well, if this sounds familiar, and you've "been there, done that," then you know exactly what I'm talking about. Equipment runs by technical rules, specifications, and guidelines based on scientific theories that you use to find and resolve the problems. People aren't quite that predictable or easy to troubleshoot. People come with different educational backgrounds, families, emotions, past experiences, and personal motivations that require more than a moment or two to assess and work with proactively. This isn't a psychology book, but its ideas are based on behavioral theory. It is a resource that will offer you ideas on how to bring out the best in people and increase the efficiency and effectiveness of your project!

The fact is that it's rare to find a project that doesn't include and depend on people, the end users in particular. Companies say that people are their greatest asset—that's really what *The Project Management Workbook* is about. By sharing a spectrum of project management options, as this book does, you will be exposed to new *possibilities* that help you bring out the best of *what is* in that wonderfully dynamic asset called "people." This is the key to successful project management, and the purpose of this book.

HOW TO USE THIS BOOK

Take a commonsense approach to using this book! Make it work for you in any way that helps to achieve your project goals. You may only need one section's information to enhance your project, or you may need many.

This book is meant to give you *options*. It explains *what* they are, then provides you with sample worksheets, ideas, and stories to show you *how* to accomplish them. Different situations and different budgets require different solutions. *The Project Management Workbook* lists and explains a spectrum of options so that you can find new tools to apply at *your* location, on *your* project.

The sample worksheets are meant to be just that—examples. There are multiple ways to design and implement worksheets. The examples give you a place to start.

Experiences, stories, and case studies are used to illustrate both "how-tos" and "lessons learned."

So, here it is:

- Options (what)
- Sample Worksheets (how-to)
- Stories/Case Studies (how it really works)
- Lessons Learned (insights and "ah hahs")

Reference Icons

Appreciative Inquiry

? Since Appreciative Inquiry may be new to you, a page at the end of each section is devoted to A.I. questions,, and how to apply it toward the topic.

Stories and Case Studies

Stories and case studies help you understand the process as it really happens. They explain things in a more meaningful and practical way while answering the question, "How does it really work?"

Lessons Learned

This is where lots of the *insight* will be shared with you. These lessons should help you to minimize potential mistakes.

High-Impact Ideas

These are the ideas that can have the most impact on your project and the people associated with it.

APPRECIATIVE INQUIRY PROCESS

The Project Management Workbook uses an appreciative inquiry, asset-based, solution-oriented approach to effective project management.

That means using the *best* of what already is (the assets in your environment) to determine what *could be* (the possibilities for your project), and what *will be* (realistic solutions for your bottom line).

This is referred to as the *Appreciative Inquiry Approach* because is uses the positive questioning process to identify your assets, on which you then build. (See the Appendix for a more detailed explanation on what Appreciative Inquiry is.) Examples are provided in each section.

Too often people look at situations as problems to be solved rather than as avenues to create new possibilities. We *often* overlook and underutilize the assets we already have. The potential is already there—this book helps you tap into it in greater depth.

The Project Management Workbook will help you discover and utilize the assets within your available resources. By building partnerships, you can create new models for successful project management.

SO HERE'S THE STORY

Background

The manufacturing facility of this case study looked like this:

- The parent company was eight billion dollars in size, this being the largest of their plants.

- The facility was over a million-and-a-half square feet, built in the early 1950s.

- It employed approximately 2000 employees, with some literacy issues. Employees spoke five languages, although most understood English.

- The average seniority was 25 years, the average age 49.
- There were three unions, with relatively cooperative working relations.
- There was a full range of technology, from very old to very advanced.

The Situation

Technical Focus

Being number one in the industry was a status that the company maintained with its high-quality products, as well as by staying on the cutting edge technologically. Installing new equipment and systems was a main strategy for remaining competitive, which meant that there were many ongoing capital projects throughout the network of plants. The typical project consisted of a project team made up of headquarters' engineers and local staff from manufacturing, engineering, and maintenance. Other support groups were brought in when needed. The HDQ project leader and engineers and a local project manager selected and purchased the equipment, coordinated the use of contractors, and managed the installation and start-up. They conferred with the production and maintenance management staff throughout the process. The focus was about 95 percent technical. See Figure 1.1.

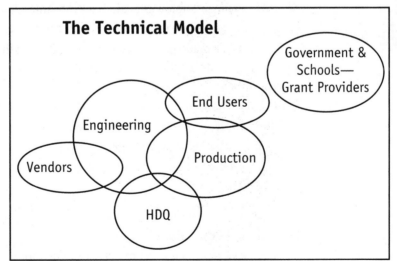

Figure 1.1 Using the technical model, engineering is the center of activity and the only group that interfaces with almost all of the other members of the project team.

They typically:

- Arranged for training as an afterthought (prior to installation) and with little or no input from the location's personnel.
- Included support groups only when they needed them (or when things weren't working).
- Had manuals or documentation that were not written at the proper level for end users, or, just as bad, had no written materials at all.
- Had installation manuals, which were written for and by engineers, that lacked any of the insight customization required by the project, often making them useless to most end users.
- Had service reps trying to install and train at the same time.

Complications

Using this approach, things got done, but not as effectively as they could have been. Projects were often overbudget and late. Many of the problems that continually surfaced were the following:

- ✔ Each person had an individual agenda. Support groups didn't have an understanding of the big picture, and they felt used. (They didn't have a common goal, which made teamwork difficult.)
- ✔ Little documentation was available for training, as a reliable resource for troubleshooting, or as an operating reference.
- ✔ Training was inadequate and often took place on the fly. This required end users to do a lot of trial-and-error learning, which lead to much frustration.
- ✔ Insufficient training resulted in low skill levels in end users. This lead to downtime, excessive overtime, delayed start-ups, material losses, and overdependence on costly vendors.
- ✔ Vendors were not held accountable for the training, so the return on that investment was very low.
- ✔ Blaming and finger-pointing were commonplace.

Resolution: Adding the People Focus

Recognizing that our capital projects could be more effective, we set out to improve the process. The opportunity presented itself when we were granted a $55-million capital project—the largest project at this facility. We decided to increase the focus on the people side of this capital project, so the technical side would be more effective. (See Figure 1.2.) The best equipment in the world is virtually worthless if the end users don't know how to use it. These are the steps we took, which had significant impact:

✔ Long before equipment was selected, we put a *technical training task force* together. This multifunctional team, consisting of engineering, maintenance, HR, and purchasing, designed a draft of *training and documentation specifications*. The draft was presented to focus groups throughout the network, as well as to the vendors, for their input. This included hourly employees too—*very important*!

✔ We *invited vendors* from around the world to a meeting to share our overall training expectations and gather their input about the training specs draft. They eagerly attended and appreciated being asked for their input. We openly discussed their suggestions and concerns, stressing that we would collaborate to find win-win solutions. We also reinforced the importance of training by letting them know that it would become a part of the *bid packages* submitted to purchasing from then on. This was the beginning of a true partnership arrangement! Expectations were well defined and mutually agreed upon.

✔ We conducted a *training and skills needs assessment* to identify the social and technical skills that would be needed in order to make this project a success. Since we were making cultural changes with new job designs—team-based line, multitasking—we had to pay close attention to how these changes would affect the employees. With this information, we designed a *comprehensive training plan* consisting of pretraining and start-up training. The pretraining consisted of team skills and basic technical skills, like keyboarding, basic Programmable Logic Controllers (PLCs), basic robotics, etc. These were *key* skills that were needed before they could understand the specific training provided by the vendors.

✔ We also developed our internal capacities by training *hourly facilitators* and *hourly technical trainers*. This is one of the most long-term and effective initiatives to take. It built internal strength, and created ownership and accountability, while reducing our dependencies on external resources, with bottom-line cost savings everywhere! We were also able to secure substantial *grant money* to support our training expenses! Another *key* is that we had a *training coordinator* to make the whole process work.

✔ We built *partnerships* from the beginning with a "kickoff" meeting attended by the core project team, vendors, and support departments, including hourly employees. It's critical that everyone gets the big picture from the start. The *hourly employees*, in particular, have so much knowledge and experience to contribute—they can make or break a project! We included them during all phases of the project. They even worked at the vendors locations, for short periods of time, to understand the equipment better and to become cotrainers with the

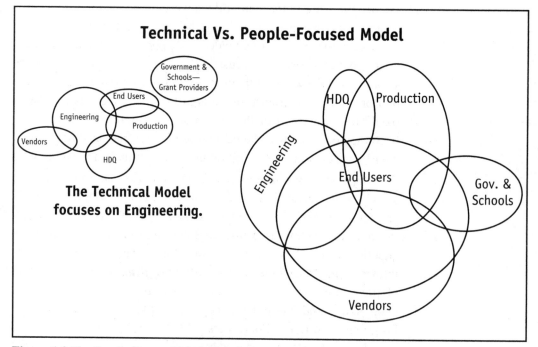

Figure 1.2 The People-Focused Model keeps the end users as the center of the project, encouraging their involvement at all steps of the process.

vendors.

Projects are much more successful when the people are:

✔ Included in the planning
✔ Trained sufficiently
✔ Given the proper tools

Project Management Results

	Technical Focus	Technical PLUS People Focus
Ownership	Engineers and production mgrs.	Key stakeholders—vendors, hourly staff, support departments, engineers, end users
Planning and designing	Engineers and production mgrs.	Key stakeholders—vendors, hourly staff, support departments, engineers, end users
Documentation	• Written for and by engineers for standard models in technical jargon • Late or insufficient • Not at users' level	• Jointly developed specifications • Developed user-friendly materials for end users, at their level, in layman's terms
Training	• Set up by engineers • No expectations • No evaluation • No accountability	• Training needs assessment completed • Developed pretraining for both technical and social skills • Training coordinator sets up training schedules • Expectations identified and evaluated • Trainers and training evaluated • Grant funding
Trainer	• A service rep, who was also installing • Someone who may not have instruction on training skills	• Rep dedicated to training • Training rep selected by team • Rep cotrains with internal staff • Internal trainers
Vendors' role	• Buyer/seller—somewhat adversarial	• Partner • Common goals
Results	• Overdependence on service reps • Insufficient training leads to trail-and-error learning • Lost time due to skill deficiencies • Little or no return on training investment • Frustration and blaming • Raw and finished-goods losses	• Developed new bid process to include training up front • Built partnerships • Developed internal capacity • Cost savings due to accelerated start-up (reduced time by 50 percent) • Reduced dependence on vendors • Improved training model • Grant support

Show Me the Money

Okay, fine, you say, but what you really want to know is, *what were the results*? Here's a summary of the main results—the bottom line!

- Reduced start-up time by 50 percent.
- Saved over $500,000 due to the accelerated timeline.
- Reduced dependency on vendors for service calls.

    (At one point, no outside service reps were called for over three months.)

    This was a substantial savings!

- Received $180,000 in grant money to pay for a good portion of the training.
- Developed internal capabilities through trainers and a team-based line.
- Significantly improved the training and documentation model.
- Developed a more cooperative, *win-win* vendor partnership!
- Built ownership into the staff as they became empowered—morale improved tremendously!

This was such an exceptional experience with so many lessons learned. Some *high-impact* lessons were:

- Partnering with the vendors and asking for their input was very helpful. Their appreciation was long lasting, and their actions showed the support we needed. It's so important to emphasize the fact that you are both working toward the same goal, and to discuss what that goal is. Everyone wants to succeed!
- You must be realistic with vendors and show that you will collaborate with them to meet the expectations. Smaller vendors may feel that they just can't afford the added expense required by higher expectations. We were aware of that and offered many alternatives that would still meet our needs at a reasonable cost. It's advantageous to demonstrate how these higher standards can also become their own competitive advantage, leading to higher sales.

- Some vendors thought we meant that they had to redo everything they had. We quickly assured them that we would start with what they had, find any gaps, and then jointly find a solution. This helped to ease their minds tremendously. We also told them that we knew it meant their bids to us would be higher—we knew we had to absorb some of the cost.

- I can never emphasize enough the importance of involving and developing your hourly staff. The hourly internal facilitators taught all of the team classes, which built in ownership for the change process. The technical trainers cotrained with the vendors, then assumed the training responsibility once they were gone. This built our capacities while reducing the dependence on vendors.

- Without a training coordinator, whether part-time or full-time, the likelihood of all of these advantages coming to fruition is reduced *sig nificantly*. This person does so much nitty-gritty coordination that makes things actually happen. The core project team of engineering and operations have many technical details to attend to, so it's not fair or effective to expect them to take on the training too.

- Never underestimate the power of building partnerships. They satisfy many of our most basic needs—feeling important (self-esteem), being a part of something (socialization), and the need to achieve. When you give people the opportunity to build partnerships *or* to get involved *or* play an active role, you're sure to make tremendous gains in anything you do.

- Remember and reinforce the fact that you all have the *same goal*. The vendors want their equipment to work so they can sell more. The company wants the equipment to work to meet their Return on Investment (ROI), and the people want the equipment to work so their jobs flow smoothly.

- Blaming or pointing fingers helps *no one*!

- Trust is an important element—it must be earned. Openness helps!

- Your hourly labor force is often the most untapped resource—use it!

If you are thinking...

"That's nice, but I have very little money and resources for *my* project, so none of these things applies," I hear you. My goal was to show you an example of how a project can be done right when adding the people focus and the resources to support if. *But* ... you don't have to do all of these things to improve your project. Even if you do *one thing* differently, you'll see results! Now that you know about the possibilities, your job is to pick which ones can benefit you!

SWOT ANALYSIS

One tool that can be very helpful in your project planning is to do a S.W.O.T. analysis of your project and project team. A SWOT analysis helps you identify *up front* what your Strengths, Weaknesses, Opportunities, and Threats are so that you can develop a plan to ensure that you use the best of what you have to eliminate or reduce the threats and weaknesses. This should be done with your crossfunctional project team at the start of the project. Follow this by preparing a SWOT worksheet, Figure 1.3.

Project XYE

STRENGTHS	WEAKNESSES
OPPORTUNITIES	**THREATS**

Once you've completed this, develop your plan by filling out the SWOT analysis worksheet, Figure 1.3, identifying how you'll utilize the best of *what is*, and how you'll reduce or eliminate the weaknesses and threats. Thinking in Appreciative Inquiry terms, you're creating a plan that turns what *could be* into what *will be*!

?

- The strengths are the best of *what is*.
- The brainstorming about how you could use these strengths to overcome the weaknesses and threats or build on the opportunities is what *could be*.
- Putting those ideas together with reality creates what *will be*.

Actions	Responsible	Accountable	Consult with and/or Inform	Target Date
Strengths				
Weaknesses				
Opportunities				
Threats				

Figure 1.3 SWOT worksheet.

13

2

Getting Started

BEGIN WITH THE END IN MIND

To use the words of Steven Covey, the second of his seven principles is, "Begin with the end in mind." The most obvious place a project starts, from a project management standpoint, is with the development of the *Capital Appropriation Request* (CAR). Each company has a different but similar name for this. The CAR is the written justification for the project. It requests the following information:

- Description of the present situation.
- Recommendation for improvement (proposed solution).
- The Internal Rate of Return or IRR (justification).
- Payback.
- Net Present Value (NPV).
- The projected cost. (This includes equipment capitalized and expense items, including training, that can't be depreciated and affect the Profit and Loss.)
- *Lots* of signatures of approval!

It's important to note that capital projects include safety, sanitation, governmental regulatory requirements, and basic improvements just to stay in business—not just technological upgrades.

The *cost* and the *IRR* are critical when approving a project; the *budget* is critical when you run the project, but the success of the project is measured in the *start-up*. Using a collaborative approach, with engineering, to select carefully and design the installation ensures lower costs by a factor of four dollars saved to every one dollar spent on engineering. *The same applies to people and start-up.*

Use the budget as one of your guidelines in using this book. In determining what options will be appropriate for your project, you'll need to know what your budget is, as well as the project objectives. It's important when you are developing the CAR to think about the *people side* of the project. Too often, it's addressed too late to ask for more money or additional resources.

The people side, in projects, typically refers to the training necessary to upgrade the skill sets of those who will operate and maintain the equipment, process, or facility being submitted for the project. Take the time to estimate training expenses.

The next few pages will give you an example of how to calculate that number. Once you have that information, you can focus on the options in the book that fit your wallet. But remember, it's about more than just money. In the project objectives, you may be introducing new ways of organizing work that require cultural changes or union involvement. It's important to know about those elements *before* you submit your CAR, so that your estimates are as inclusive as possible, and you can accomplish your objectives.

Other benefits from a collaborative planning approach upfront are:

- Reduction in ergonomic-related injuries (risk prevention)—a collaborative design can build a high quality of work-life environment and prevent costly redesigns.
- Reduction of product warranty liability—training can reduce injuries, especially during start-up, and reduce consumer complaints and law suits due to product contamination.
- Reduction of "Lost Opportunity" costs—those costs that build up because people aren't trained (such as overtime, material losses, etc.).

With that said, it's also realistic to say that *often you can't get everything you want*. Don't let that deter you from doing the right thing when it comes to people—*there's always a way!* This book will give you options, but it's also meant to encourage you to use your imagination to create the best project results that you can, through effective people management.

Another possibility—aside from the traditional project budget—is to explore the availability of *grants* to apply for. That is covered in more depth later under "Finding Grant Money" in Chapter 4.

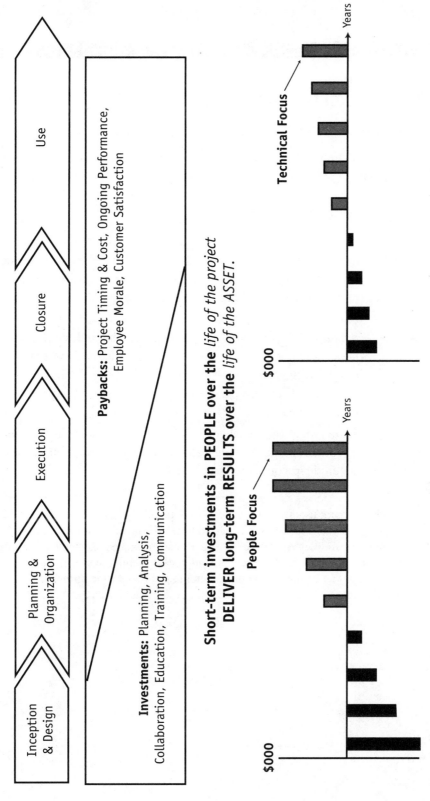

LIFE OF A PROJECT

Inception & Design	Planning & Organization	Execution	Closure	Use

Investments: Planning, Analysis, Collaboration, Education, Training, Communication

Paybacks: Project Timing & Cost, Ongoing Performance, Employee Morale, Customer Satisfaction

Short-term investments in PEOPLE over the *life of the project* **DELIVER long-term RESULTS over the** *life of the ASSET.*

People Focus

$000

Years

Technical Focus

$000

Years

Figure 2.1 Project IRR and NPV are driven by the timing and size of cash flows. Will YOU make the RIGHT investments?

DIGGING FOR DETAILS
GETTING INFORMATION FOR YOUR C.A.R.

Call Your Vendors

Your vendors know their equipment and processes, and the skills it takes to operate, repair, and maintain them, better than anyone else, so talk to them and get as much detail as possible.

The best approach is to:

- *Identify* the best people to speak to about training on their equipment/process. (Often your sales rep may not be as knowledgeable about the training as someone else within the company.) Try the head of the service or training department.

- Prior to your call, develop a *letter of introduction* and a short *questionnaire* for your vendors to complete. This will help them do the legwork in finding the details you are looking for. Fax or email it with a note saying when you'll call to follow up. Include your email address and fax number so they can send it back to you as soon as they complete it.

- *Know* what you want. (This will be covered in greater detail in Chapter 7, on developing training specs.) The form on the next page should help you with this.

Vendors are not usually in the business of training, so they won't always be as thorough as you'd like. Don't be afraid to ask for the details. If they don't have training capabilities, you'll need to find other resources. Remember, you both have the same goal—to have equipment/process running to spec in order to produce a high-quality product process—training can make the difference!

VENDOR LETTER OF INTRODUCTION

1235 W. Client Lane
Lansing, IL 60555
July 10, 2002

Vendor Contact
Vendor Name
Vendor Address

Subject: Project XYE Training

Dear..........,

We are currently in the process of developing our capital request for Project XYE. We have actively been involved in the review and selection of your equipment as a primary vendor for the project. Based on our discussions and observations, we look forward to the excellent technology you have to offer to the success of this project.

The purchase of your equipment/process will require new skills for our operator and maintenance staff, which means that we'll need training support from you. We would like to capture that cost now so we can include it in our capital request. I've enclosed a short questionnaire of the information that we'll need in order to estimate costs, and I will call you within a week to follow up on this information. If you are able to complete the information prior to that, please fax it to me at 333-777-9999.

I appreciate your assistance in gathering this information and look forward to an excellent working partnership with your company.

Sincerely,

TRAINING QUESTIONNAIRE

Training Questionnaire (for vendors)

Company Name/Address	*Training Contact*
	Name
	Phone
	Fax
	Email
	Cell Phone

- What equipment/system are you providing? (brief description)

- List the technical skills required to operate/troubleshoot/maintain this equipment. (Ex., basic reading skills, PLC experience, etc.)

  Be as specific as possible!

- Operate:

- Troubleshoot:

- Repair & Maintain:

- Do you have training staff to train our operators and maintenance staff? (If not, how do you usually provide training to your clients?)

- Will your training staff be able to train on any shift? (If not, what are the limitations?)

Describe the training capabilities that you can provide to this project:

(Check off those you *have* and *can provide*)

Manuals that include:

- _____ Installation procedures
- _____ Safety
- _____ Operating procedures
- _____ Troubleshooting guides
- _____ Maintenance procedures
- _____ Preventive Maintenance (PMs)
- _____ Parts list
- _____ Other (describe)

Instructors _____

Job Performance Aids (JPAs)

- _____ Checklists
- _____ Troubleshooting guides
- _____ Specific procedures
- _____ Diagrams
- _____ Evaluation performance checks

- Do you have a training catalog, or a list of training programs you offer? _____

   If so, please mail it to the address on this letter.

   Do you have any training resources on the Internet? If so, list the Web site address.

- Do you have a training center where your courses are held? _____

   If so, where is it located?

- **Would you consider having one, or more, of our employees visit your facility during the building of the equipment (as a part of training experience)?**

Thank you for taking the time to fill this out. Although I will be contacting you individually to discuss this in more detail, feel free to fax it to me at ......

Thanks for partnering with us!

?　　　　*Training Questionnaire—Follow-Up Phone Questions*

---

1. Describe the most successful training that you've seen conducted with your equipment/process. (the best of *what is*)

2. What made this so successful?

3. What did your company and your client do that was different than most training you've seen?

4. What do you need from us to create the same (or better) kind of positive experience? (what *could be*)

5. Do you foresee any barriers to the success of the training here? If so, what can we do to eliminate or reduce them?

6. Given the resources and possibilities we have, what is the best possible scenario that we can create? (what *will be*)

7. What other ideas, questions, and/or concerns would you like to discuss with us?

ESTIMATING TRAINING COSTS

The components to think about when estimating the *training cost* for your project, are:

- Vendor Cost
- Labor Hours
- Training Documentation/Materials

Vendor Cost

Vendor cost should be negotiated when the purchasing discussions are in progress. Although equipment/process is the core expense, service and training are *critical* and should not be ignored at this time. You should have prior guidelines from the purchasing department, and build training expectations into the contract. In relation to training (this usually pertains to service also), there are several ways that a vendor may charge:

How They Charge

Training Contact Hours

- Daily charges, by trade
- Hourly charges, by trade

Either of these is typical and realistic

Training Noncontact Hours

This usually pertains to vendors that aren't local.

- *Door-to-door rate for noncontact hours

Try to avoid the door-to-door—it's very expensive.

Expenses

- Per-diem rate for travel expenses (lodging + meals) + coach air fare
- All, at their cost

It's best to set guidelines.

Total Project

- Charge for project completion cost

Usually, they don't like to do this for training because of the uncertainty and risk, but depending on the size of the project, it may be to your advantage. *All these are ways of charging for training services and are a part of the negotiations.*

Door-to-door means that you pay for the trainers' travel time, as well as their training time. Travel time is from the time they leave their house until they arrive at their destination—either the hotel (if they are from out of town) or your facility. If they do charge "door-to-door," it should be at a lower hourly rate than the contact rate.

Typical Scenario

If you don't know what to ask for, vendors say they will do training, and send very brief proposals, if any. They usually don't ask for many details about your needs, or they add training time on as "service time," and don't distinguish it in any way. Too often, it isn't even considered until installation. Often their idea of "training" is to show someone something while they are installing and hope that it takes. This is the cause of poor start-ups, downtime, expensive service calls, and overdependence on vendors. (This will be covered in greater detail in the Chapters 5, 6, and 7.)

To avoid these scenarios and create new, more positive ones, here are some questions that you should be asking yourself:

Labor Hours

To estimate their labor hours, for the actual training, you need to answer these questions:

1) How many people need to be trained? (List the numbers for each group.)

Number of People to Be Trained			
Type	*1st Shift*	*2nd Shift*	*3rd Shift*
Operators			
Mechanics			
Electricians			
Electronic Technicians			
Supervisors			
Stationery Engineers			

It's important to separate them because you need to ask for training by type. For example, if you had 20 mechanics, you need to ask:
- Will the mechanics be trained separately, or with another group?
- How much time will their training take?
- Do you have an outline of the course content?

(Each group requires training unique to their job responsibilities.)
You'll need to ask this with every type of person to be trained so you can estimate the hours correctly. If vendors are vague, give them a brief overview of what you want them to teach the employees. You can actually develop your own matrix or checklist for each type. This helps all of you focus better. *You're more likely to get what you want if you ask for it.* The vendors may not like your attention to detail, but it will pay off later on—for both you and your vendors.

Content Matrix
Here's an example of a Content Matrix.

Training Content Matrix						
Check off the topics that should be included in each type of employee training.						
Topic	*Operator*	*Mechanic*	*Electrician*	*Electronic Technician*	*Stationery Engineer*	*Supervisor*
Systems/Equipment Overview						
Safety						
Tools & Parts						
Installation						
Start-Up						
Operating Procedures						
Shut-Down						
Troubleshooting						
Repair & Maintenance						
Other						

2) How many *people* (by type) can be away from the floor, per shift, at any one time, for training? (This is to determine number of repeat sessions needed.)

- Operators _____

- Mechanics _____

- Electricians _____

- Electronic Technicians (ETs) _____

- Stationery Engineers _____

3) Can trainees be trained on any shift? (There may be union issues.)

4) Will the vendor trainers be willing to train on any shift? If no, when can they train?

5) What is the maximum group size (by type) the *trainer* will be able and willing to train at one time? (You need to know this to decide how many repeat sessions you need to conduct.)

- Operators _____

- Mechanics _____

- Electricians _____

- ETs _____

- Stationery Engineers _____

Training Documentation

Training documentation usually means *training manuals and job aids*, or the *development of training documentation*. This can be done either by the vendor's training staff or by a third-party external training vendor. It can be subcontracted by either, but usually you would be doing the subcontracting. This is where it's important that you have training specs!

Training Manuals and Job Aids

This is quite easy to cost if they are already developed. It's simply the *price of the manuals or job aids* × the *number of copies* you need. Make sure you review them before purchase to ensure that they are useful and written at the end users' level!

Training Documentation

(The difference between manuals and documentation is that documentation is developed from scratch to meet the specific needs/specs of the client versus standard manuals. It can be customized manuals, job aids, etc.)

This is much more complicated and costly. The value, of course, is that you get high-quality materials that meet your exact needs. They usually can be provided in an electronic format too, which is easier to update. If you do request electronic copies, make sure that they are on the same platform you are using; otherwise they are useless!

If you are having a third-party vendor develop manuals and/or job aids, you need to:

- Allow time for the third-party vendor to talk to both the equipment vendors and the internal resources. (Again, the training specs are important here.)
- Allow time for a proposal to be developed, which will include the labor hours for development, travel expenses, and duplication costs. This often is difficult to have completed by the time the CAR needs to be completed. That may mean you need to develop another CAR just for training documentation.

COST ESTIMATE WORKSHEET

Vendor Cost

- *Contact Hours*

Number of sessions × number of hours × cost per hour =

Total Cost for training contact hours _____

- *Noncontact Hours* (door-to-door)

Number of hours × cost per hours =

Total Cost for noncontact hours_____

- *Travel Expenses*

Air fare, hotel, car rental, food, misc.

Total Travel Expenses_____

- *Training Materials*

Manuals, job aids, videos, CD ROMs

Total Training Materials _____

Total Vendor Cost Estimate for Training _____

Labor Cost (for hourly trainees)

Number of staff × number of hours in training × loaded* rate per hour = Total Cost of hourly labor for training

*(Loaded rate includes base pay + benefits)

Total Hourly Labor Cost _____

You will probably need to calculate this by type of position because each position will most likely have a different rate of pay. Labor costs typically aren't calculated for salaried employees.

Training Documentation Cost

This can be as simple as the cost of manuals or as complicated as the cost for a training vendor (either the company from which you are purchasing the equipment or a third-party vendor). They would submit a proposal that would include their total cost (labor, travel, and replication).

Figure 2.1 Cost Estimate Form—Guidelines

COST ESTIMATE SAMPLE	
Vendor Cost	
• **Contact Hours**	
Number of sessions × number of hours × cost per hour	
5 sessions × 4 hours per session × $75/hr.	
Total Cost for training contact hours	**$1500**
• **Noncontact Hours** (door-to-door)	
Number of hours × cost per hour	
8 hrs. × $40 **Total Cost for noncontact hours**	**$320**
• **Travel Expenses**	
Air fare ($400); hotel, 2 nts. @ 90 ($180); car rental, 2 dys. @ $45 ($90); food ($60); misc., parking at airport, 2 dys. @ $15 ($30)	
Total Travel Expenses	**$760**
• **Training Materials**	
Manuals, job aids, videos, CD ROMs	
20 manuals @ $20 **Total Training Materials**	**$400**
Total Vendor Cost Estimate for Training	**$2980**

Labor Cost (for hourly staff)	
Number of staff × number of hours in training × loaded* rate per hour = Total Cost of hourly labor for training	
15 operators × $30/hr. (loaded) × 4 hrs. in training each = $1800	
5 maintenance staff × $40/hr. (loaded) × 8 hrs. = $1600	
Total Hourly Labor Cost	**$3400**

Training Documentation Cost (Optional)	
This can be as simple as the cost of manuals or as complicated as the cost for a training vendor (either the company from which you are purchasing the equipment or a third-party vendor). They would submit a proposal that would include their total cost (labor, travel, and replication). Ex. **Document Development Proposal $20,000**	
TOTAL Training Cost Estimate = **$26,380**	

Figure 2.2 Cost Estimate Form—Sample

APPRECIATIVE INQUIRY APPLICATION

? *Chapter 2—Getting Started*

In Chapter 2 We Discussed:

- How to work collaboratively with your vendors to identify their training cost
- Sample questionnaires
- Identifying what all the training costs are
- How to estimate your overall training cost for the CAR
- The life of a project

How Was Appreciative Inquiry Applied?

- Finding the *best* people to give you the *best* information (from the vendors), and discussing what support they could provide, was a start. That sounds simple, but if you talk to just anyone at the vendor's company, that person may not be aware of what is actually available. If you don't know what the vendor's *best* is, you more than likely won't get it.
- The main illustration of AI here was in the follow-up phone call questionnaire, through the use of these types of questions:
  - Describe the most successful training experience you've conducted/seen.
  - What was it that made it successful? What did you do differently?
  - What do you need from us to create that same kind of positive training experience?
  - What is your strongest asset while training? (Manuals, trainers, job aids, etc.)
  - What support can we provide that will enhance your training?
- With this information, you can build on what they are capable of (best of *what is*), brainstorm how to use what was learned from their best experiences (what *could be*), and what you can do with what resources you have (what *will be*).

NOTE: We are looking at the positive, and building from there—not trying to be adversarial. Questions are always the starting point for AI.

Remember, questions are just the *start* of Appreciative Inquiry. To create your better future you *must* take the answers to these questions through the what *could be* and *will be* steps.

QUESTIONS TO ASK ABOUT GETTING STARTED

Internally

- Who will take the responsibility for employee training and its coordination?
- Is training a part of the original CAR? If not, find out how to ensure it is.
- Has project money been allocated for training?
- What training models have worked in the past?
- Is there any money available within the local budget, or will it all have to come from the capital project budget?
- Who is usually responsible for developing the training budget?

Externally (Vendors)

- What training capabilities do they have? (The questionnaire will help you with this)
- Can we see samples of their training materials and resources?
- Do they have off-site training facilities?
- Do they allow clients to train at their facility?
- Who is the best person to speak to about training?
- Who conducts the training?
- Are there references to call to get more information about their training capabilities? (It is probably best to do this later—once you start to design the training plan.)

> As a project manager, or engineer, these questions need to be answered *before* the CAR is completed. Otherwise, you can be assured that you won't get what you need to support training for your project!

THE APPRECIATIVE INQUIRY PROCESS—SAMPLE APPLICATION

To help you understand the AI process, as it might be applied to this training situation, here is an example of what might take place to create their vision of a positive training environment. (This is merely a simple outline of the steps and how they might be utilized.)

Step 1: The BEST of what is

To identify the best of *what is*, you develop questions that will draw out *positive*, *appreciative* stories or examples. In the case of training, we could ask:

AI Questions

- Describe a time when your training produced exceptional results. What contributed to those results?
- When you think of your training assets, what would they be? What does the organization do best?
- Describe a time when you were really excited about going to training.

Although these are just a few example of asset-based questions, you can come up with many more based on what you are targeting to create, enhance, etc.

Some answers to these questions might be:

- When the instructor was well prepared and listened to us. The respect made us want to learn.
- When I actually had the time to *do* what we were learning and get feedback on it. Feeling good about my progress was great!
- When the instructors got us involved and knew what they were talking about.
- We have great internal trainers—they know us and all our needs.
- We have a great training resource who supports us—the training manager.
- I couldn't wait to get to training to learn this new skill that would make my job easier.
- I loved it when I could choose the training that supported my professional growth—then once I completed it, I actually got to apply the new skill to my job. I really felt proud mastering it.
- I loved getting a certificate of completion.
- I loved when the instructor let me coach another trainee because I had picked it up so easily. It made me feel important and smart, but most importantly, I liked helping.
- I felt very proud to be selected to go off-site to a special training class where I got to meet people from other locations. We shared and learned so much from one another.

Step 2: What could be

Now knowing the best of what already is, what you value, begin to *imagine* what *could be* that takes you a step beyond. Think of new possibilities. Be brave here, even outrageous in thinking what you want the future to be. You are creating the positive image of what future training will look like. Even if it's just identifying one thing that will made a big difference...go for it!

This is the time for *open dialogue*—get all the ideas out. You're building a training vision. In the case of projects, you should do this together with partners. Gather those responsible for training from the vendors, along with internal training representatives, making sure the end users are involved. Ask the questions above to both. You'll see that each partner has different strengths that probably compliment one another nicely. In this *imagining state*, join those together. Get the best of both! Once the ideas are voiced, write statements that describe your new vision of training. Select the one that energizes you the most and embodies what you value. We call this your *provocative proposition.*

Provocative Proposition

As PARTNERS, we will identify what training is needed and the best way to deliver it, utilizing both the customer and the vendor within each step. The delivery will exceed learning expectations because of the total involvement, and the results will create attention as a model and receive appreciation from all.

Step 3: What will be

Now that you have your vision, look at your realities and identify what can and will be done to enhance your future training. Here's a sample:

(Even if you just choose one of the following ideas, you'd be making progress.)

With all future training relationships we will:

- Build a partnership agreement in the initial stages of the relationship, setting specific goals and expectations.
- Have Purchasing add this expectation to the contracts, making it a way of doing business.
- Always have end users be a part of the total training process.
- Develop a training team of internal trainers—making them our core training resource.
- Identify what we valued in each training experience so we can continually enhance our processes and results.
- Share our successes so others can learn from them.

Key Points

✔ Your provocative proposition should *energize* those whom it will affect.

✔ What you decide you can and will do, from the energy of the provocative proposition, doesn't have to be a huge new project or a major change. It merely has to be something that can make a difference, no matter how small it is...something that brings hope and embodies what you value the most.

✔ One of the true beauties of the process is that you are working from what is known—it's already been successful. This helps to reduce the typical fear accompanied with any change.

3

Developing Partnerships

PARTNERSHIPS

Partnerships are the *key* to any successful project. There are at least four main partnerships that need to be built.

- Project Team (cross-functional)
- Vendors/Suppliers
- Internal Staff (including end users)
- Governmental/Educational Agencies

Taking the time to build these partnerships will *dramatically* enhance the end results of your project and make your project life a lot easier! In this chapter, we take a look at each group and give you a number of ways to build effective partnerships, using the appreciative approach, and building on the *best* of what is!

Project Team

The project team is usually a cross-functional group of internal staff that is responsible for the planning and implementation of the capital project. This internal team may include staff from other locations (such as headquarters), contractors, and associated staff from quality, HR, engineering, maintenance, production, accounting, sanitation, and whoever else is appropriate. It can be a fairly large group (over 10) that has varying roles and commitments to the project. Few participants will be committed full-time; most contribute on an as-needed basis. It's fair to say that many, if not most, of the team members are also still responsible for their full-time jobs. At times, the project manager and engineers are working on multiple projects. It's important to understand the various time commitments and levels of participation. With that said, let's take a look at the not-so-golden rules of project management, so we know what we're realistically working with.

THE NOT-SO-GOLDEN RULES OF PROJECT MANAGEMENT

- Putting people together on a project team does not automatically create a team...*you know that, right*?
- You more than likely won't get to pick your team. Chances are that they will be picked for their expertise and availability, *not* their ability to be effective team members.
- Murphy's Law tends to apply to projects, so be flexible and prepared for many changes. Schedules and plans exist to be changed. Contingency plans are a *must*.
- Just when you get the engineers who really understand the new equipment/system and accelerate your progress, they will get reassigned to another project somewhere else.
- Time lines and targets change for a million reasons, most of which you don't have control over...but you're still responsible for!
- You don't always get the equipment/process you want—it may be a political decision. Common sense doesn't always prevail.
- You usually won't get all the money you want! (Really, have you ever?!)
- You may do all the work but not get the credit when it works, but you can count on getting all the credit when it doesn't!
- Budgets get redistributed more frequently as the project progresses or regresses.
- People love to claim that it's always someone else's fault.
- The more vendors that are involved, the greater the complexity of communication issues, especially where control systems and programming are involved.
- The end users tend to get left out until it's installation time—way too late!
- Whoever works the hardest gets the most to do! (If you want to get something done, ask a busy person.)

Knowing all of these "rules" and *accepting them*, if you can't change them, is an important starting point. No matter how much you wish this or that, wishing doesn't make things happen. That's just how life is. Your job is to see things and people as assets, not liabilities or problems to fix. By finding the *best* in what you have, you can build new possibilities that you may have overlooked before. Your actions and attitude do make *all* the difference!

Looking at the Best of What Is!

- *You* can control yourself and your approach!
- *Everyone* on your team has expertise that can help the project along!
- *Everyone* wants to succeed, as well as be a part of a successful project!
- *You* can create new possibilities using the appreciative inquiry approach—just by asking the right questions.
- *Everyone* needs to be respected—it only takes a little time and effort.
- *You* can build success into the project process.
- Having fun makes a difference, and helps get your team through the tough times!
- Just like Maslow's Hierarchy of Needs—there is a hierarchy of needs for projects too!

PROJECT TEAM'S HIERARCHY OF NEEDS

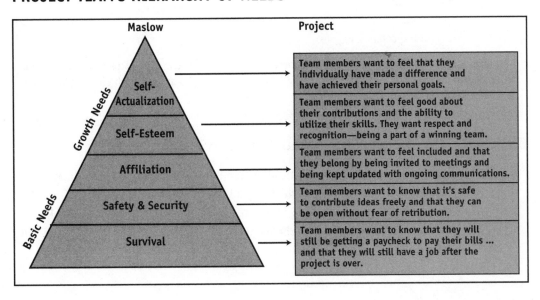

KICKING OFF YOUR PROJECT

Involve everyone *from the start!* Sounds simple, but so often team members get brought in just when they are needed. This doesn't make them feel too committed, let alone very important. Effectively solicit their buy-in from the beginning.

One of the best ways to get off to a good start is to have some sort of team meeting, lunch, or gathering, to get them together. The members want to know three things:

- What does the overview of the project look like (why, how, when, etc.)?
- Where do I fit?
- What are my roles and expectations?

All of this is *very simple* and critical to building ownership and accountability. No one likes to hear things after the fact. It's great to include vendors and end users too, if you can accommodate them.

To prepare for this meeting:

Get nice folders and pens—if possible, have them customized with the project's name on it. Make this their project team "toolbox." Include in it:

- Project Overview
- Project Time Line
- Team Members List
- Roles and Expectations

Add information continuously, as it becomes available, like the members' phone list, updated information, checklist of "to do's" etc. Hand info out at meetings and through email. This toolbox should be brought to all meetings.

BUILDING THE PARTNERSHIP—PROJECT TEAMS

Here is a variety of possibilities that can help your teams! Start with an *appreciative, asset-based* approach! Hold a kickoff meeting, with food, if possible (food attracts participation), at a convenient location. Send out a "ticket" as the invitation, with the agenda and a simple request. This is their "entry" into the meeting.

You're Invited

What: "Kick-off Meeting"—Project XYE

When: July 30th—11:30 a.m.–1:30 p.m. (lunch provided)

Where: Conference Room D

Agenda: List by time and topic

Admission: Fill out this ticket by answering these questions!

Admission Price: 1) Tell me about the *most successful* project team (or *any* team) you have been on. What made it successful? (25 words or less), and 2) What do you think your role is on this team?

You can use this during the Project Operating Principles portion of the meeting (see next page), to start a brief discussion about how the team members want to work together. All of these good experiences can then become the model for what *could* and *will be* your operating principles for the team. This asset-based approach sets the stage for positive dialogue rather than gripes about why they dislike project teams or problems they've had before! Find someone good in facilitation skills to do this—perhaps an HR person or the project team leader.

Project XYE Kick-Off Meeting Agenda—July 30, 2002

11:30–Noon   Lunch and Introductions

Have a sign-in sheet to get everyone's name, backup person, phone number, fax number, email address, current position, and mailing address (if needed). Create a team list with this information and distribute it with meeting notes within a few days of the meeting. Everyone should introduce themselves—name, job, their role on the team, and what skills they bring to help the team. (If this is too much, some of this information can be discussed later, as noted below.)

Noon–12:30   Project Overview/Critical Success Factors

This should include why the project is being done, the mission, dollar value, known target dates, and any other pertinent data available. Allow for questions! Jointly identify the Critical Success Factors. (These are the critical things that your team needs in order to succeed.)

12:30–1:00   Project Operating Principles

Ask everyone to share their most positive and successful project team experiences (admission ticket). Put these qualities on a flip chart. After each member has shared, read from the chart list and discuss which ideas you want for this team. Put these operating principles on a sheet and have members sign it. Have open discussion on how the team can ensure their utilization. Along with this discussion, you can ask each person these follow-up questions (if you haven't already during the intro portion). These help everyone become more familiar with one another's strengths and motivations.

- Why was this experience personally rewarding?
- What role did you play?
- What way do you think you can contribute the most to this team?

This may sound like a lot, but it can go pretty quickly. If you are going to ask these other questions, it's a good idea to let the team members know in advance. You don't want to surprise or embarrass them. Give them the right to pass.

1:00–1:15   Roles and Responsibilities

Some of the most important things that the team members want to know are, "what do you want from me?" and "where do I fit?" It's worth the prep time to have a list of participants and describe briefly what role they will play, which may be provided by each person ahead of time. By reviewing it with the group, additions or changes can be made. Include it in their toolboxes. Participants will appreciate this.

1:15–1:30   Next Steps and Questions

This is self-explanatory, but *very important*!

Project XYE Team List

Here is another approach. Send this information sheet out with the meeting invitation. Ask that it be returned two to three days before the meeting. From this information, assemble a team list that can be included in the project toolbox. This can accelerate the meeting's progress.

Project XYE Team	
Name: Company: Address:	Phone: Fax: Cell Phone: Email Address:
Current Position: Boss' name:	Your Project Backup: Name: Phone:
Briefly answer the following questions, as best you can.	
Describe your most successful project experience. What made it successful?	
What role and responsibilities do you think you'll have on this project? Role: Responsibilities:	
How do you think you can contribute to this project? What special skills/strengths do you want to utilize?	
Please fax or email this to....... At 333-444-5555, no later than July 27th. We'll use this information so that we can have a team list for you at the meeting on July 30th.	

Possibilities

- **Hold the kickoff meeting at an outdoor site with a short team-building "outdoor adventure" portion to it.** This doesn't have to cost much. Many local park districts are doing this now for $10–$25 a person, or for a lump fee. They will lead the group through some fun team exercises, then debrief the group. Nothing builds teams faster than putting them into an environment that's new to them and

PROJECT TEAM LIST

Name	Contact	Address	Role	Backup	Boss
Company Members					
Jim Morris	312-777-4422 312-777-4420 fax 312-777-5432 cell morris@xyz.com	7733 Broadway Chicago, IL 60606	Project Eng Packaging	Sally Field 312-777-4484 fields@xyz.com	Josh Brown Eng Mgr 312-777-440 brownj@xyz.com
Sue Cooly	201-888-4444 201-888-4448 fax 201-889-9090 pager	3320 Long Street Sansong, NJ 20010	Commercialization HDQ	Sam Winters 201-888-7342 winters@xyz.com	Barb Collins 201-888-4433 collinsb@xyz.com
Vendor Members					
John Jones	714-543-2121 714-543-2100 fax 714-542-2231 pager jonesj@jamesc.com	54000 Sames St. Buffalo, NY 66040	James Manufacturer Sales Rep	Julie Hassel 714-543-7657 hasselj@jamesm.com	Julius Morris 714-543-7575 morrisj@jamesm.com

Figure 3.1 Project Team List Sample

taking them out of their normal roles. This levels the playing field—everyone is equal. It relaxes people and gets them to talk more freely. This can be done in half a day. If done in the afternoon people will tend to hang around afterward and get better acquainted, getting them off to a good start.

- **Use symbols.** Many teams have some sort of team symbol. It may be the T-shirt, a key ring, a team folder, a special pen, or a pad of paper that can be used at the team meetings. It doesn't have to be expensive—just fun and meaningful. If you do get something engraved, make sure to allow plenty of time. It could take two to six weeks.

- **Celebrate Successes.** Set milestones. Measure and communicate them! You may want to use the SMART approach, making goals **S**pecific, **M**easurable, **A**chievable, **R**ealistic, and **T**imed. Again, it could be as simple as pizza, or rolls and coffee, or going out to dinner, having a picnic, etc. You may want to use the United Way idea. Have some symbol (an arrow, an hourglass, a picture of the product or process that the equipment or line will be making) and color it in as you make progress. Make this visible—perhaps by the new area (line, process, or piece of equipment) or in the cafeteria, or wherever it will be seen, to let everyone know you're moving forward. Or just shade in the progress, in green, on a Gant chart.

- **Set expectations** from the start and continually reinforce them. Redefine them, as needed. At the kickoff meeting, give everyone their own team folder with the project's mission, time line, roles and expectations stated, and any other pertinent data. Request that they bring those folders with them to each meeting. Call it their project "toolbox."

- **Show personal appreciation.** Take time to say "thanks," in person (which is the best), or through email or some other communication vehicle. Use your newsletter to show progress and successes, or create a separate project email newsletter.

- **Have fun monthly drawings** for those who attend the meeting. Prizes could be a small gift certificate, the company's product (if appropriate), tickets, or even just silly prizes. You could even have one fun one and one nice one. You could have each team member be responsible for the drawing prize, for one meeting, but set limits. They could use it to give "antique" items from their department—yep—fun stuff!

- Have a traveling prize for best effort of the week, or wildest blunder, or best story. Maybe that is a broom or a bike wheel or a ball. Use your imagination! Make it fun but *don't make it time-consuming!* Give each department a role in these prize and drawing ideas. Fun keeps morale up and teamwork strong!

- Try the **Open Space** technique when it seems like people have a lot on their minds but they aren't expressing it (in the group, anyway). This allows for good, healthy discussion. (See the next page for full details.) Open Space is a "free form" group-generated agenda that can be very productive because people talk openly rather than sitting in a long project meeting waiting for their one topic of interest to come up. The key to this format is to set some time guidelines so the discussions can be to the point. Try it—it's something they probably haven't done before. The openness may bring out some disagreements, but that too is important to team growth. Remember "forming, storming, norming, performing" is the growth cycle of a team. The storming is critical to growth; just make sure that issues get resolved.

- Invite marketing in to give everyone on the project team an update on the product. They often add some excitement to the team process and let the team know more about the marketing plans. It's good for marketing to get out to the plants and see what it takes to execute their plans. They often may have fun giveaways too. This tends to energize the team and makes them see the end goal, in real terms.

Open Space Technology

Open Space Technology is a technique that Harrison Owen originated purely by accident. It's a more effective way to hold meetings/conferences. He is a public market maker, academic and biblical scholar that, at times, conducted workshops with groups. He noticed that the most activity and productive interaction happened during the breaks, when people just freely exchanged their thoughts and interest. So for one workshop in India, rather than prepare extensively, he let the group decide what they wanted to talk about. From there this process was developed and is now used extensively.

Materials Needed

Four to eight pieces of paper (cut or rip a piece of flip-chart paper into four pieces), marking pencils/pens, masking tape.

Instructions

(This is an abbreviated version.)

- Everyone who wants to talk about something (in this case, related to the project) takes a piece of paper and writes down that topic. They put their names on the bottom.
- When the four or eight pieces all have topics (or however many get filled—it could be fewer) on them paste either one or two on each wall. (Assign a time to each topic so participants know when the topic will be discussed.)
- Tell the group members to now go to the topic that they want to talk about. Set a time for each discussion period, e.g., no more than 20 minutes. If you have eight topics, call "switch" when the first round of discussions should change. Only do two rounds, with no more than four topics being discussed at any one time. Gauge this by the size of your group. (Longer sessions would have more rounds.)

The Rules

1. The *Two-Foot Rule* states that if you aren't getting anything out of the group that you chose, get your two feet up and go walk to another group.
2. The *Bumble Bee and Butterfly Rule* says that you can either be a bumble bee and talk in the group or cross pollinate by going to other groups carrying information to them, or you can be a butterfly and just hover in the group listening quietly.
3. No one gets offended if people *move in and out* of groups. The point is to get the information you need, and that everyone takes responsibility for their own learning/information gathering.
4. The discussion *begins* when it begins and *ends* when it ends. The point here is not to prolong something any longer than needed.

5. Whoever *wrote the topic* sits in that topic discussion. The discussion is always informal and open. You set the time guidelines to meet the project team's needs. Notes should be taken and made available to all.

For more information on Open Technology read *Expanding Our Now: The Story of Open Space Technology*, by Harrison Owen (or any of his other books) or checkout www.tmn.com/openspace.

VENDORS

The first step toward building a partnership with your vendors/suppliers is with your mindset. If you can remember that you all have the same goal, that will help tremendously. Get rid of "I'm the boss, just do as I say." Remember that they are no different than anyone else. They want to understand their role and be involved—that's the way they can be most effective...just like you! You may be the boss/customer, but you need their cooperation, skills, and expertise to accomplish your goals. Know their skills, and utilize them wisely!

The old saying, "you catch a lot more flies with honey than with vinegar" still holds true! Here are some ways to do that.

✔ If they are "preferred vendors," involve them in the planning team. They may have excellent ideas to contribute to your design—ones that could save time and money. They will feel good about your trust in them and will be committed to contributing.

✔ Invite them to the kickoff team meeting. Let them give a *brief* introduction of their product and services. Since most team members only have a piece of the project, this will help to give everyone a broader understanding of the whole project.

✔ Hold a separate vendor kickoff meeting to get them acquainted with the project team, as well as the other vendors with whom they will be interfacing. This is especially true for systems and programming suppliers. Many projects get held up by the problems caused by having different programmers whose systems don't talk to one another. Make sure you cover expectations—theirs and yours—at the meeting, rather than just assuming what one another will do. Take this time to clarify expectations by asking the vendors what they need! Tell them what you need. Tap into the *best* of *what is*—theirs and yours. Apply A.I. here. Your final list should include the common goal, expectations of vendors and clients, and the definition of success from both. Develop a Partnership Agreement. (See Appendix for sample.)

✔ Ask for their opinions and insights from their past experiences. The vendor meeting we held to talk about training expectations, discussed in Chapter 2, was successful because no one had previously ever taken the time to ask them for their input. They are used to being told. Any relationship is improved greatly when opinions are *asked for, listened to,* and *respected.* A great deal of synergy can evolve!

✔ Give them feedback and appreciation when they have demonstrated true commitment and have attained good results.

✔ Identify your expectations of one another at the beginning, and refer back to that agreement whenever issues arise. Decide in the beginning how you'll resolve differences.

E.g., We once invited "Inspector #5" to our facility to say "thanks." It seemed that our operators kept noticing every time this certain packaging material was inspected by #5 it was always good, unlike other inspectors. Because of this person's efforts, we invited Inspector #5 to be a part of a problem-solving team (quite an honor for an hourly inspector). Then, while on the team, we presented him with an award for his great work. We also took a picture to put in both our newsletter and theirs! This was simple but a real win-win!

END USERS

If I could, I'd like to have this whole section on end users highlighted, bolded, underscored, and emphasized in any way possible. I can't overemphasize enough how very, very important this partnership is...and how rewarding it can be!

I want to highlight it because of all the relationships needed to make your project work, this is the one that gets the least attention and yet has the most underdeveloped potential. Without their support and involvement, your project has a slim chance of success! They can make or break your project in the long term!

When the project team has disbanded, it's the end users who have to make it work. When I say end users, I include:

- Operators
- Mechanics
- Electricians

- Electronics Technicians
- Stationary Engineers

Really, it's *all the hourly people* (operations people—their titles may be different in your workplace) who make the line/equipment/process run, and the people who *supervise* them! The *real* people don't get to walk away when the project is done. They hold all that life experience that isn't in any book. They know the idiosyncrasies of the process, the people, the equipment, and the product, which only they can know. They also know the shortcuts that do and don't work.

They may not always have much formal education, may not be able to read or write well, may not speak the language, but they are going to make your project work, or not, in the end. It's time to spend more time and money developing them as your most valuable asset by working with the *best* of what they do have. You will see the results very quickly!

Involvement

Here are some possibilities to build the *end users* partnership... Invite hourly* (operations) staff to the kickoff meeting. Get them involved from the beginning! Make them a permanent part of the project team!

Select and train *hourly trainers* who become the Subject Matter Experts (SMEs) for the new equipment/system/process.

Let them join engineers/project managers on *site visits* to look at *potential suppliers* of equipment and/or a process. Get their insight as to how that equipment might work (or not) at your location. They will ask great questions that will help in your selection!

Once the equipment/process is selected, *send a representative* down to the equipment/process *vendor's location*, for a short period of time, to participate in the building of the equipment or process. This will give the person first-hand knowledge of the operation and repair of the equipment, while building a close relationship with the vendor. This goes a long way toward developing internal skills/capacities and end user partnerships. It also allows that person to be a cotrainer when the on-site training is conducted. This is an excellent and productive perk for the hourly trainers.

Select hourly representatives, as appropriate, to be on any *task forces* that are developed—like the development of training specifications, development of training plans and courses, etc. Their insight and ideas will be invaluable in ensuring that you develop what *they need*, not just what *management* thinks they need!

Whenever possible, on-line and off, bring them into the conversations that will affect them.

*When using the term "hourly," it applies to anyone paid hourly—union members, nonexempt or technician level, depending on the industry.

There are so many stories that demonstrate the impact of good end user partnerships, it's hard to just pick a few.

- When we were designing a *"pay for skills" program* for one union, we had a *joint labor-management task force* that developed the guidelines, the program content, and the implementation. Once the managers on the committee were able truly to let go and empower the hourly staff, progress jumped by leaps and bounds. Not only did the hourly staff help design the classes, but they assisted the outside vendors (who were conducting the classes) with all the details, including designing the simulations used, selecting the instructors, and developing the evaluation procedures. They even made a decision to appropriately fire an instructor. They took over all the scheduling, which often is quite a challenge, making sure that there was no reason for anyone to miss a class, while still covering the production floor.

  The outside providers were paying close attention to what they delivered—classes had never been so effective and so well coordinated to our needs. This carried over into capital projects since they already had such success working with the outside vendors. Our hourly staff actually taught them a lot, which they then applied to their teaching methods! Training was at its best when they took such an active part! Hourly staff then began to teach the classes themselves.

- To receive adequate training on control systems, which are so prevalent in capital projects, simulators are critical to the learning process. One craft group had a lab, but many of the parts had been "borrowed" to help out during equipment failure downtime. To remedy that, the craft group rallied around, made a list of what was needed, then worked with the engineers and maintenance management to locate replacements. They quickly found them within the facility, and the lab was operational again...and it didn't cost them anything except a little time! The synergy to accomplish their goal was impressive.

- When implementing the *first team-based line* at a midsized plant, the hourly staff team determined what was important to them—what operating principles/values they wanted to guide them through this new line experience. After much discussion, they agreed on 10. They then put them on a sheet of paper with a symbolic border. On the border, they signed their names to demonstrate their commitment to this team contract. These 10 principles were then developed into the core training components of the team development process.

  The really interesting part was that they then requested different members of management and the project team to come to their meetings to give presentations. Once they worked with each of those individuals, they shared their principles and requested that the presenters add their signatures to show their support. It became a status symbol for the management team to have their names attached to it.

  To ensure that it became a part of the daily way of doing work, they each had a copy posted in their lockers, a larger version of it on the wall by the new line, and in the training and conference rooms where they met. Any violation of the contract was a part of the "lessons learned" and a growth opportunity.

LESSONS LEARNED

- Whenever you empower the hourly staff, they will far *exceed* your expectations!
- You must show trust to get it back. Remember that mistakes will still happen—look for the best in people, and build on it.
- Your project payback goes far beyond the life of a project when you've built a strong partnership with the end users. They will continue to share their thoughts and ideas, beyond the project life.
- You build tremendous commitment and loyalty when you take the time to develop these relationships. It takes very little—just some *genuine* interest and the ability to listen. Don't pretend!
- Always remember to give feedback to the end users' ideas—if you disagree with an idea, ask questions. Don't blow them off.
- If you ignore their ideas, or don't respond, forget ever getting their cooperation and/or ideas in the future. They will just let things happen, even when they know they are bad, from then on.

EDUCATIONAL AND GOVERNMENTAL PARTNERSHIPS

Governmental Partnerships—Federal, State, Local

It's always to your advantage to develop positive governmental relationships. They can be a primary outside financial supporter of your projects through training grants and other resources/incentives. Even if grant money may not be available when you apply, they can refer you to other agencies or educational institutions that may have funding. By keeping an ongoing dialogue, your name and needs will be on their minds when grants come up.

Here Are a Few Suggestions:

- *Invite the appropriate person out to visit your location.* Government staff usually enjoy getting out and becoming more familiar with what needs exist. During their visit, share your success stories, your company's community involvement, and any past positive experiences with agencies. It's something they won't know if you don't share it. The government's responsibility is to keep in touch with its communities' needs—this gives them a firsthand opportunity. Likewise, they will be sharing useful information with you.

- *Keep your involvement in any agency or nonprofit organizations visible.* Use your newsletter or bulletin boards to keep your employees aware of community involvement. Refer and encourage them to volunteer for programs. There may be opportunities to work with an adopt-a-school program, coordinate a walkathon, hold a blood drive, etc. Demonstrate that your company is a good community citizen.

- *Become a resource.* When we received literacy grants and implemented a model program, the state often referred others to us for advice. We then partnered with the state in many ways—giving presentations, being on a grant-reading team, hosting literacy panels, etc. They got to know us and respect our contributions. This wasn't time-consuming, either.

- Don't be afraid to *call for help* and/or ideas. They have many resources and are usually very enthusiastic about sharing them! These resources are our tax dollars at work—find and use them!

Educational Partnerships

Many of the governmental suggestions apply to schools too, but here are additional recommendations.

- *Visit their location.* Find out firsthand what facilities and resources they have. Schools, especially community colleges, have a wealth of programs, grants, and ongoing initiatives that are there to support you and your company!

- While visiting, *meet as many people as you can* that may help you understand and see the spectrum of what they have to offer. Usually, there is a business institute within both community and regular four-year colleges and universities. These are your *key* resources because it's their mission to work collaboratively to meet the needs of the business community. These institutes have a database of instructors and Subject Matter Experts (SMEs) to support most any need you may have. They offer both traditional and custom-designed programs.

- *Volunteer* to be on their *advisory board*! Timewise, it's not usually demanding, but the benefits for you, your company, and the school are abundant. The objective of these boards is to tap into your insight and experience to identify ways that the schools can be effective and active partners in meeting your company's and community's needs.

- *Ask about what grants* they have and if any could be applied toward your company's project. If they don't have any, ask for other suggestions. They may be aware of a grant that they would be willing to help you apply for.

- If you do have a *grant partner* with a school, make sure that you are always *actively involved* in the process. Schools are always learning from you, and your company, about how to be effective contributors. If their staff has no industrial experience, you need to make sure that they understand your unique needs and how to address them. Although they may know about the adult learner, they may not be familiar with the amount of flexibility that is required from a scheduling and course-content side.

Because of the strong relationship we had built with our community colleges, they would actually call us when they had grant money to see if there was a fit. Schools have to spend the grant money or they lose it, just like individual companies. Losing grant money reduces the potential for funding in the future. This is something they always try to avoid.

APPRECIATIVE INQUIRY APPLICATION

? *In Chapter 3 We Discussed:*

- The importance of partnerships and the types required for projects
- The not-so-golden rules of project management
- The Project Hierarchy of Needs
- Project possibilities
- Specific ideas for each type of partnership

How Was Appreciative Inquiry Applied?

This section was full of examples of A.I.

- By including vendors and end users in planning, you solicit their positive input—asking them for good past experiences and examples. This helps to find what worked and what we should do more of (the best of *what is* and *what could be*).

- In the kickoff meeting example, we asked everyone to identify what they could contribute and what skills they'd like to use most—we were looking for the best of what they had to offer. Their skills and interest may go beyond what their traditional role is. Knowing this helps to build what *could be*. Often, people don't volunteer this information unless they are asked because they don't know if anyone cares.

- By brainstorming with all those associated with the project—especially from the beginning—you use your assets (your internal staff) to find all that's available to you and your project's success. Again, by identifying the best of *what is* (assets), you can then collaborate more positively about what *could be* (your ideal), and then get to what *will be* (the realistic but broader capability).

Remember, questions are just the start of Appreciative Inquiry. To create your better future, you must take the answers to these questions through the "what could be" and "what will be" steps.

QUESTIONS TO ASK ABOUT PARTNERSHIPS

Vendors

- Invite the vendors to visit your facility to get an overview. Ask if you can visit theirs, and if employees would be welcome to train at their site.
- Ask who will be doing the training, and ask to see the materials/formats that will be used.
- Ask them to develop specific training goals with you.
- Ask what they need to conduct effective training successfully.

End Users

- If there is a union at your location, sit down and discuss the technological changes (and cultural, if there are some) with the union leadership—to give them the full picture and get them involved in the design/training, etc. Ask for their ideas. (Work with HR on this so you understand the contract and any other past practices.)
- If there is no union, ask HR to help you understand which employees will be involved, what barriers you might experience, and what you have to do to get them involved.

Governmental Agencies

- Ask what governmental agencies may have grants available and if there are relationships already in place. Who are they? Who could be the person to assume this responsibility? HR? Manufacturing? Purchasing? Accounting? All of these?
- Ask who internally could write a grant, if needed. Do you have a grant writer already?

Educational Institutions

- Ask what local educational providers could help with your project.
- Ask who could follow up, get catalogs, and talk to their contacts.

4

Finding Grant Money

SO WHERE IS THE MONEY?

Federal, state, and local governmental agencies are valuable sources for workplace training grants to help fund your projects. They usually fall under the category of *economic development*. States are always in competition for new industry as well as retaining their current tax base from industry—big or small! Providing grant money is one way they can do that.

Currently, when companies are exploring new sites to start or to expand their businesses, they frequently look at the educational resources and the geographic profiles that exist in that state or city. This tells them whether, if they were to build or relocate to this area, the education/skills would be available to satisfy their staffing needs. It would be a waste of time and resources to move to an area where they would have to train all the people from scratch. Because of this, states encourage continuous skill upgrading with incentives in the form of grants.

Training Grants are usually available for one or all of the following reasons:

- To attract new industry
- To upgrade the skill sets of a company so they can remain in business
- To help the expansion of a business

- To support a TIF* designated area
- To improve literacy skills

The Logic Is Simple

- New industry and business expansion brings in new jobs and new tax money—*economic development*!
- A company that must upgrade its skills to keep up with technology might have to close if there were no financial incentives available, meaning a loss of tax revenue.
- A TIF* area, by definition, is usually an area not conducive to growth. It may be deteriorating or have become an unattractive location for financial reasons (hard to attract workers, poor transportation cost, etc.). Being designated a TIF area brings the infusion of many incentives that will revitalize the area and the business—training dollars for skills upgrade is just one of those incentives.

---

*TIF stands for *Tax Increment Financing* program. It was developed to eliminate blighted conditions found to be present in some industrial, commercial, and residential areas. The TIF program provides financial assistance to stimulate private investment in the area, to upgrade it, and to attract new development. Not all cities and states have this, but may have something similar.

GRANT BASICS

Grants not only make good economic development sense for the government; they make good business sense for you and your company. They are a vehicle to help you achieve a business goal requiring the upgrade of skills of your *incoming* and/or *incumbent* employees. To help you focus on your business need, ask yourself these two questions:

- Do our current or incoming employees have the skills to perform the necessary tasks required in the workplace? (This is an important question that you'll be asking while doing the needs assessment described in the next chapter.) Typically, a project introduces new technology that will help you identify specifically what skills will be needed to help you answer this question.

- If not, how can we acquire those skills most effectively and efficiently to reach the proficiency levels we need?

If you answer the first question by saying "no" or "not quite," your company may be a good candidate for a grant.

Basic Terms

To help you understand the information in this chapter, it's important that you're clear on what some of the terms mean.

- *Basic literacy* refers to math, reading, writing, and oral proficiency in English.

- *ESL* stands for English as a Second Language. It refers to those whose native language is not English. They often may be able to speak English but not read or write it. In the workplace, it's becoming more important that they can speak, read, and write to communicate effectively to complete their work tasks.

- *ABE*—Adult Basic Education refers to education provided in the basic literacy skills—reading, writing, math, and oral proficiency in English.

- *Literacy partners* refers to anyone who provides the basic workplace skills training to your employees. It could be an educational institution, a nonprofit organization, or a professional association.

The training provided from a grant is for workplace skill development and is typically conducted *at the workplace* to address specific workplace needs, often triggered by a project. It may be done in a classroom or on the job. Grants may fund basic literacy classes in order to prepare employees to benefit from future technical skills training, or they may fund the actual technical training (SPC, blueprint reading, computer skills).

It's important to know that workplace training can not be reimbursed *until* a grant has actually been awarded to you, and it falls within the grant time line.

LOOKING IN ALL THE RIGHT PLACES

Since each state is different, there isn't just one contact, number, or Web site with this information. Here are some ideas to get you started.

Literacy Grants

These typically cover Adult Basic Education (ABE) classes and English as a Second Language (ESL) classes.

- Department of Education, Washington, D.C.
- State Department of Education
- Secretary of State's Office
- Community colleges

General Information about Literacy Grants

These grants are usually small ($1–15 thousand) and, as most grant money is, are meant to be "seed money" to get a program started at your location. Federal grants are much harder to obtain but have a higher dollar value. If you are a large company with many field locations, it can improve your chances to apply jointly for federal funding. Likewise, if it is a state grant and all the locations reside in that state, you also have an advantage.

Economic Development Grants

These grants tend to be larger and cover companies' growth needs, as mentioned on the previous page. Here are some of the most common names and organizations where these grants can be found.

- State/City Department of Economic Development
- Employers/Industrial Training Program
- Chamber of Commerce
- Small Business Administration
- National Alliance of Business
- Your Local community college's Business and Industry Department

Additional Resources

Although the above agencies will be your primary resources, you should also consider the many employers' groups, professional organizations/associations, and not-for-profit community-based organizations (CBOs) that are highly skilled in providing customized training. Some recognized CBOs that may be in your area are Jewish Vocational Services, Urban League, and Catholic Charities, to mention just a few. Even if they can't help you, they can usually refer you to additional resources.

TWELVE THINGS YOU SHOULD KNOW ABOUT GRANTS

1) Grants are usually meant to be "seed money," to get a company started with a program or process, which they then continue on their own.

2) Grants nearly always require "matching funds" from your organization. They *never* pay for everything! Often the company's "match" is in labor hours, wages, etc., not necessarily in company dollars.

3) Grants are almost always *government sponsored*, which usually means there is a lot of paperwork involved, although there are some exceptions.

4) Grants require *detailed* administrative implementation.

5) Grants usually require some sort of *application* or *proposal*. They can be as short as 1 page or as long as 60 pages. Rule of thumb— the more money you can get from a grant program, the longer the application process will be.

6) Usually, grants follow a *financial cycle* that will be tied into the government's fiscal year (July–June). This means that often there is only one submission date a year. This is not always true, but be aware of dates when you call for information. Once you've submitted a proposal, it may take a long time to get feedback. Ask up front what the waiting period may be!

7) Grant providers usually set *limits* on an organization's ability to reapply year after year for the same grant.

8) Grant *criteria* may change. One year they may be willing to reimburse for training labor hours only, another year for only training provider cost, and so on.

9) Grants rarely pay for *hardware*—they may pay for computer education but not for the computers themselves.

10) Grants often require an educational *partnership provider*, usually a local community college or community-based organization. Typically, the grant money is kept within governmental agencies (state schools).

11) Don't assume that services provided from a *community college* will be cheaper or better than from any other potential educational provider.

12) Grants usually are for a *one-year period*. If you don't use the grant money, you'll lose it. Typically, you submit invoices or reports monthly for reimbursement once training is underway. Most grants don't give you money until you spend it.

YOUR NEXT STEPS

✔ *Call the agency and community college's Business and Industry Department* in your state/community that could be a grant provider. Explain what your company's needs are up front to introduce yourself, find if there is a match, and set the stage for future contact and the following questions. This will help you find out right away if their potential funding is appropriate for your company. It will also make the provider aware of your interest so that when your grant proposal comes to them they will already be prepared for it.

These are questions to get you started:

- Do you provide workplace training grants? If so, what do they cover, and how do I apply? If not, are you aware of where I might be able to get that information?
- When are applications due?
- What are the eligibility requirements to obtain a grant?
- What amount is available?

You may want to check *www.info.gov* on the Internet.

✔ *Attend a bidder's conference.*

Many grant providers conduct a bidder's conference where they describe the grant's purpose, bidder's qualifications, and application procedures. These preproposal conferences are often *required* before your bid/proposal can be considered. It's important to attend these. You'll not only gain valuable information, but also you'll meet the people who coordinate the program and ultimately may be making the selection decisions. Those first favorable impressions you make with them can be very helpful in attaining grant funding.

✔ *Review and complete the application (or outsource to a professional).*

If the grant application is too lengthy for you to complete, consider hiring a professional grant writer. They will usually charge you a percentage of the grant received, which can be up to 20 percent, but it's money you didn't have before. They also know the politics of grant writing and submission. You may find that your community college, if they would be the partner provider, may provide that service or already have grant money that they can apply toward your company. This saves a lot of time! If you are writing the proposal, make sure that you follow the guidelines *exactly* as directed. Failure to do so may result in your request's being disqualified from consideration.

✔ *Don't give up if you're rejected—keep applying!*

No matter what the reason for rejection—timing, quality, etc.—if you aren't awarded a grant, the exercise you went though will help you next time around. Keep trying! Ask the provider to share the reason why your proposal was not accepted. This will provide you with valuable feedback that can help you on your next proposal. Always handle rejection graciously. They will remember your negative responses!

✔ *Be detailed in the administration of the grant.*

Once you do receive grant money, be very detailed in your administration of it. They usually want proof of dates, names, dollars spent, and most importantly, results! Assign one person to take this responsibility. Most grants allow you to apply grant money to pay someone to do this. USE IT!

LESSONS LEARNED

- Apply for grants as soon as you are aware of the possibility that you may be eligible for one. The wait is often long and may disqualify you by the time you get an answer. *Always ask when you can expect to be notified.*

- Writing long grant proposals can be very time-consuming. If you don't have the time or expertise, find a professional grant writer. Because grants can be political, professionals often have the right contacts to get your grant approved. They usually have excellent insights that can make the difference in obtaining a grant or not. Negotiate the fee, because sometimes they are quite high.

- Ask grant writers for references from other companies that they have written grants for. Call these companies and get evaluations on their proposals.

- If you do hire a professional grant writer, make sure that this person *accurately* describes you in the proposal. Some use boilerplate proposals and don't always spend the time to describe you honestly. Be comfortable with what the professional writes, or have that person rewrite it.

- I can't overemphasize the importance of detailed documentation during the administration of your grant. Grants are usually audited at the end, and you need to have "all your ducks in a row." *Use some of the grant money to pay for an administrator dedicated to the project.* This person can be part-time.

- Sometimes the eligibility for a grant may change midstream; don't be surprised if you have to rewrite it.

- Since many agencies that provide grants require an educational provider partner, sometimes you don't have to do any of the work yourself. Ask the agencies to identify some of the educational provider partners, and go directly to them.

- At the end of the fiscal year there is occasionally some grant money still available. Check back with them to see if you may be eligible for it. They don't want to lose the money, so they may be happy to help you!

> If you just do one thing differently in your project management, from the people side, try to get a *grant*—It's a bottom-line *win*!

More Lessons Learned

Grants (cont.)

- Most industrial facilities do not have literacy instructors within their staff, so they will be tapping into other resources, like community colleges, community-based organizations, or other literacy providers.

- Community colleges have come a long way in learning how to work with industry, but they still come from a traditional environment, with traditional ways that you need to be aware of. Here are a few:

- *Most schools will want to test the employees* so they can identify their current skill levels to assess where training is needed to bring them up to the proficiency level required. Although this is very logical, you *must* be sensitive to the employees. To give a formal test to someone who hasn't been to school in many years, and is fearful of the class to begin with, is counterproductive. This often deters employees from attending. I was once offering literacy classes—something new to the facility—and over 90 people signed up. The educational provider insisted that we administer the Tests of Adult Basic Education, TABE Level D test, before they could provide the appropriate instructors. This test was three hours long, so we lost two-thirds of the potentially interested employees, who didn't even show up at that point. Once the tests were completed, the educational provider then wanted separate classes for every two reading levels. Not only would this require many classes, but replication of each class for all three shifts. This was very unrealistic and costly. We finally got the educational provider to agree to approach testing differently—with a much shorter test administered *after* the employees had been with the instructors a few times and their comfort level was higher.

- Many schools *require a minimum number of participants* before they will conduct a class. This often is difficult to achieve. Look for a provider who is flexible to meet your specific needs.

- Most schools want to use their *standard materials* rather than develop job-related materials. These often seem uninteresting to the students and are not the best use of your money. I'm happy to say that more customized and work-related materials are becoming available. Encourage the use of the facilities' common materials, like MSDS sheets (Material Safety Data Sheets), quality procedures, checklists, time cards, benefit materials, etc. One approach that worked well too was to have the students create the materials with the instructor. The involvement is a very positive learning experience and enhances comprehension tremendously.

- *Get involved with the selection of the instructor!* Too many instructors have a very difficult time handling the flexibility required in industry and get frustrated easily. Find out if they have taught in a workplace environment, and check references. The teacher makes *all* the difference.

- *Instructors have a hard time with accountabilities.* In business, people have very specific standards, production requirements, and quality and safety specifications that get measured daily. Teachers tend to be, and work, very independently. If you give them specific expectations, they often feel uncomfortable and unable to attain them. The main reason why this is so difficult for them in the business environment is because of the students' constant need for their attention. Employees grow very dependent on and friendly with the instructors. Instructors enjoy the attention and their ability to offer advice, which is so encouraging for employees. The problem occurs when the employees take advantage of the instructor by spending too much time just wanting to chat. Instructors should never shun students, but they have to find a balance between achieving the goals you establish and having conversations with the employees. This is their most difficult challenge. It is also a challenge for supervisors because sometimes employees try to get out of work, using the excuse that the teacher wants to see them. Negotiate specific outcomes/competencies that will be attained by the class, in your initial discussions, so there are no misunderstandings. Commit these to writing. The use of pre- and post-tests is one of the most effective ways to do this. These are important results that will be needed for the grant follow-up.

- *Be aware of the options when hiring an instructor.* This can save time and money.

  - *Go directly through the educational institution.* This is usually charged out by the hour and can be very costly. They may also do it by the project, but it still may be at the hourly rate.

  - *Go through an educational provider* that puts your instructor on their payroll and charges you the *salary* (not an hourly rate) they pay them. This is usually the most cost-effective method, but you need to find an organization that bills this way. It usually works best if you find the instructor yourself, have the provider in the interview loop, then have the educational provider hire the instructor. You will be billed for the salary, which is much cheaper than an hourly rate.

  - *Use an independent contractor.* This will only work if your instructor is also working for other companies/people as well as your company. You need to be careful not to violate the *independent contractor guidelines*, which say the instructors cannot be independent contractors if they only work for you and you determine all that they do.

- *Hire the instructor as your employee.* This is also very cost-effective because you'll be paying them a salary, *but* most companies don't have the luxury of having that extra head count available. You would probably be paying higher allowances (benefits) if you hired the instructor as your employee rather than if you hired one through an educational provider that bills the instructor's salary to you.

APPRECIATIVE INQUIRY APPLICATION

? *In Chapter 4 We Discussed:*

- Where to find training grants
- Reasons why grants are provided
- Things to know about grants
- Lots of lessons learned
- Your next steps

How Was Appreciative Inquiry Applied?

When contacting governmental agencies, you will be asking lots of questions to help find what you need. Some of these can be very helpful:

- What makes a company a good candidate for grant money?
- What is the best recommendation for a successful application?
- From the grants awarded, what companies stand out as effectively using the money? Who are the *best*? Could you refer me to someone at that facility from whom I could get more information?
- If you don't have any funding available, could you refer me to the best resources that could provide additional information about potential funding?

Along with questions, use your conversations to find out more general information about how your company can be more involved in obtaining resources from the state/city. Find these people to visit and learn from. There is so much out there waiting to be used!

Appreciative Inquiry always starts with questions about the best of *what is*. This is the foundation for opening up new opportunities. From there, you can brainstorm new possibilities to create what *could be* and eventually, what *will be*. All three steps are important in order to reap the total benefits of Appreciative Inquiry. The questions listed above are just the start of Step 1.

QUESTIONS TO ASK ABOUT GRANTS

Internally

- Do we have a need to upgrade the skills of the employees to achieve our business goals?
- If so, what is the most effective way to do that?
- Has this facility ever received any outside funding/grants for workplace training? If so, from where?
- Who was and/or could be responsible for writing a grant proposal?
- Can we research the possibility of gaining training funds for this project through grants?

Externally (Government and Schools)

- Are there any workplace training grants or funding resources currently available? If so, please explain what the selection criterion is and the dollar value.
- What does the workplace training grant money cover?
- When are grants awarded, and when are the proposals due?
- Will there be a bidder's conference?
- Can you please send an application to us?
- If you have none available, are you aware of anyone else I should talk to about workplace training grants?
- Do you currently have a workplace training grant that we could be included in? (This pertains mostly to schools, educational services providers, or even community-based organizations.) Do you have any classes that we could take that would be paid for by workplace grant money? (Sometimes schools offer classes that are paid for through grants. You can apply to participate in those.)
- Once we submit a workplace training grant, when can we expect to be notified if we were selected or not? (It's a good idea to ask if you could occasionally check back with them.)

5

Identifying Your Needs

When writing your project's Capital Appropriation Request (CAR), you are *estimating* the cost as well the savings and/or benefits. Usually, the emphasis is on the new equipment or process cost—the technological part. Typically, the people side, the training in particular, is just assumed to be in the numbers, or is overlooked altogether. To avoid that, you need to identify the specifics, the real people *cost* and the real *needs* to achieve your goals, *during the planning stages*. To do this, conduct a *needs assessment*. This can be very detailed or relatively simple, depending on the scope of the project. Simply begin with the end in mind—what the goals of the project and the organization are and how those will affect the end users. But before we even do that let's review why and how we should do one.

WHY DO A NEEDS ASSESSMENT?

✔ Do a needs assessment to save time, money, and effort by *identifying* and *focusing* on the *specific* solutions to your needs—it helps you find what the right thing is.

✔ Do a needs assessment in order to target your efforts on the specific project and organizational goals.

WHOSE JOB IS IT?

You're probably asking how, when, and by whom is this needs assessment done. Who gives it, who takes it? How many people are included?

The best person to *conduct* the needs assessment is someone who can look and listen objectively, who isn't biased about what needs to be done, and who has a stake in the success of the project. A needs assessment isn't about right or wrong, good or bad. It's about targeting the business needs so you take the right actions to achieve the goals.

A Needs Assessment:

- Clarifies what you have and where you are (Current Situation)
- Helps identify the gaps
- Helps target what you need (Future Best)
- Is a foundation for planning and budgeting
- Builds partnerships and ownership

Externally, an organizational development specialist or training specialist is ideal to develop and conduct the assessment, but here are a few internal suggestions:

- ✔ *Human Resources*
  - Organizational Development Specialist
  - Training and Development Specialist
  - Labor Relations Staff
  - Employees Relations Staff
- ✔ *Quality Control*
  - Continuous Improvement Personnel
  - Quality Auditor
  - Quality Assurance Personnel
- ✔ Others
  - *Anyone who:*
    - Is a good listener and open to ideas from all levels
    - Is a person who thinks broadly and doesn't make value judgments
    - Is detail oriented and analytical
    - Has had prior project experience
    - Has a stake in the project's success

Who Should Take the Assessment?

A wide range of people associated with the end results—engineers, HR, operations, maintenance, purchasing, and *most importantly*, end users! The more people included, the more valid the results. As a minimum, each type of person should have at least three represented. (This number varies by the size and complexity of the project.)

HOW AND WHEN TO DO A NEEDS ASSESSMENT

When Should a Needs Assessment Be Done?

A needs assessment should be conducted in the *planning stages* of your project to ensure that your recommendations become a part of the budgeting and CAR process. Most of this information is considered in planning, but the details are rarely completed until later. This can result in fractured, crisis, and time-driven decisions. As the project progresses and budgets get tighter, your ability to do the right things diminishes. This will have a significant effect on the end result...and the bottom line. *Consider a needs assessment to be a tool to reduce cost and a key to any project's success*...because it is. A project without a needs assessment can be likened to building a house without blueprints.

How Should a Needs Assessment Be Conducted?

A needs assessment can be conducted in a variety of ways—for example, one-on-one interviews, focus groups, or on-line or mailed surveys to be filled out. Two components that get coupled with *all* of these methods are *observation* and *informational data*. Observations show you how things really are, and specific information gives you tangible data of what you've heard (or not) during the interviews and focus groups. It provides good information to ask about in the sessions. For example, if you notice that the third shift's safety record is much worse than the others', it's a good idea to find out why. You'll have to decide, based on your situation, which of these three approaches is most appropriate for your project. A combination of the methods is highly recommended to get the best information. No matter what method you choose, the key is to get a wide range of participation from all affected—project team, HR, end users, etc. Too often the project team makes decisions without sufficient input from others, especially the end users. *This early involvement builds a foundation for the partnership and ownership needed to make your project a success.*

One-on-One Interviews

This is self-explanatory. You determine the questions that you are going to ask, have them in a written form, schedule individual time with a wide range of the appropriate people, and conduct the interview. It can be as short as 15 minutes or as long as an hour. *Be sensitive to participants' time.* You should explain *what* you are doing, *why*, and *how* their input will benefit the project. If you can share how this information will benefit them *personally*, it will help tremendously. Ask everyone some common questions, so you'll get different perspectives, plus the questions appropriate to their roles. *Be consistent with the questions.* If you ask everyone different questions, you won't be able to see themes from which to base your conclusions and recommendations. Always allow for some open-ended questions and, *think appreciatively too, by asking about the positive*—what has worked in the past. It's a good idea to send the questions ahead of the interview so people have time to think about their answers, especially if specific data is required that they may need to look up. You'll save lots of time this way, and participants will appreciate your sensitivity to their time. On the other hand, don't be surprised if they don't take the time to read it prior to your interview. Stick to the scheduled time allotment, unless the participant wants to add more and has given you permission to continue.

Focus Groups

Focus groups are small groups of people brought together to share their thoughts and ideas about a focused topic. The groups are usually small, 5–10 people, and may be either similar or dissimilar people, depending on your needs. The reason to conduct focus groups is to save time and money, and to utilize the synergy of the group. People often forget about certain ideas until others bring them up. Ideas feed off of ideas. Watch out for dominators who may monopolize the group and the group dynamics, inhibiting other people from saying what they really feel. Sometimes people don't like to speak up in a group or they are afraid to add their opinion if it's different than others. Remember, you still need to be *consistent* with your questions.

On-Line or Mailed Surveys

Surveys are often used to save time and money, and to reach a greater number of people. If you reach more people, this typically improves the validity of your results. If you do surveys, remember not to make them too long or too complicated or participants may get discouraged and not bother to complete them. Always include *why* you are doing the survey on a short cover letter. Mention how the results will be used, and why they were selected. It's also important *to thank them for their participation* and not to require their names, so they can answer without fear of recrimination. If it's done on email, and they don't want to reveal their names, make sure a place is listed that the surveys should be returned to. *Remember to put a date that it must be returned by, as well as the place to return it to.*

Before sending out your survey, have a few people complete one (other than yourself) to make sure it's understandable and gathers the precise information that you are seeking.

ASSESSMENT TECHNIQUES

Technique	*Benefits*	*Things to Watch For*
One-on-One Interviews Interviews	• Can get in-depth input • Can ask for details and clarification of answers	• Consuming too much time • Collecting too much data • Interviewer's interpretation, listening, and questioning skills
Hints:	• BE CONSISTENT with your questions • Send questions ahead of the interview	
Focus Groups	• Can talk to more people • Time saving • Gain benefits of group synergy	• Dominators who monopolize the discussion • Group dynamics—either intimidating people or swaying the feelings to go along with the others • Scheduling barriers
Hints:	• Choose appropriate people—those that are affected by the project and/or those that can offer expert advice, also people who are interested and can offer different opinions	
On-line Survey Mailed Survey	• Can reach more people • Can do it quickly • Inexpensive	• Low return rate • May not get as wide a range of participants as needed or wanted, if return is low • Answers may be open for interpretation • May not be able to get to the depth you want
Hints:	• Make surveys easy to understand and short • Tell people why you are doing them • Always put a return date and location • Always provide feedback of results	

CAUTIONS

- Don't shortchange this process, but don't be overwhelmed by it either.
- The information that follows may seem time-consuming—the examples include the full spectrum of possible questions to utilize on your needs assessment. Pick and choose *only* what applies to your project and organization.
- When gathering specific hard-core numbers, don't waste your time requesting this information from multiple people. (I.e., safety record, head count, etc.)
- Don't take more time than you requested from individuals during the needs assessment process—respect their time religiously. If you need more information from people, ask their permission to continue or to reschedule additional time.
- Many of the questions can be answered very quickly; others may take time to calculate (numbers of people). Start with the quick ones.
- Use common sense!

On the next few pages are samples of questions that you can use. After each topic, there are parentheses around the departments that might be most appropriate for these questions to be asked of. Again, don't be overwhelmed by the length of this list. It merely gives you a wide range from which to choose. You just need to pick or develop the questions that meet the needs of your project.

BEGINNING YOUR PROJECT TRAINING NEEDS ASSESSMENT

Now that we know why and how to do a needs assessment, it's time to focus on your project needs and build your own training needs assessment tool to support it.

Begin by asking the following questions:

When the project is successfully completed, what will be different?

Technologically (most of this should be in your CAR)
- What new equipment/process/system will be operational?

- How will the equipment/process/system look once it's operational?
  - What will be the same?
  - What will be different?
- What will the end results of these changes be?
  - Productivity?
  - Cost?
  - Quality?
  - Delivery?
  - Safety?
  - Morale?
- How will these changes affect the accounting process? Quality systems? Other departments?

You must be able to identify your targeted goals clearly...so you can ask the right questions during your needs assessment.

People Side (Socio)
- How will the technological changes affect the people and their jobs?
- Do you need different skill sets? If so, what?
- Do you need different people? External versus internal? Fewer? More?
- Will end users have new or more complex tasks to perform?
- Will the changes create the need for new job classifications?
- Will it have an ergonomic impact?
- Will the communication process be different?
- Will the employees be managed differently? Will they have more autonomy?
- Will the changes require union agreement/negotiations?
- Will there be any cultural changes happening simultaneously?
- Will jobs be structured differently? Will they be paid differently? (I.e., self-directed work teams, multiskilling, pay for skills?)
- Who will coordinate the people changes? Who will be accountable?
- If people will be released because of the changes, what process will you take to do that?
- Will this impact the current management structure?

Use these answers, written in summary or matrix form, to develop your needs assessment tool. Remember, a valid and inclusive needs assessment must examine the *specific project* and *organizational goals* that the project needs to satisfy. You must be able to identify your targeted goals clearly so you can ask the right questions.

Example—Summary Form

Project goal: Increase productivity by 28 percent, reduce waste by 3 percent, improve quality by reducing product rejects to less than 1 percent, and reduce consumer complaints, etc.

Organizational goal: Become the highest-quality, lowest-cost producer in the network, and restructure work by using a team-based work structure.

Example of what your summary may look like

Technologically, the new line will have all new high-speed packaging equipment, which is totally controlled by the latest generation of PLCs and a pick-in-place robot case packer and sealer. This new equipment will increase the speed from 220 a minute to 440 a minute, with an expected doubling of the output. The waste should be reduced from eight percent to four percent. With all the new safety stops and guarding, accidents are also expected to decline. It will be operational at a specific production level and independent of external resources by the end of the year.

Socially, the line head count will be reduced from 22 to 10, but will require workers capable of doing multiple tasks. The skill sets will require at least eighth-grade reading level, basic mechanical aptitude, and the ability to communicate via the panel view screens and computer input. A new job classification will be required, which must be presented to the union leadership at a very early stage of the project. Because it is a union environment, we will need to work to develop the skill sets of the current employees rather than hiring from the outside. A selection process, including testing, must be developed and administered legally and with union support. A new pay scale will have to be evaluated also. Extensive training will be required, including both basic skills and specific technical skills. The management structure will not change, but the end users' job scope will broaden considerably because it will be team-based. They will now do 70 percent of the quality checks and conduct safety audits. Operators will do minor mechanical repairs and contact maintenance directly rather than through supervisors.

Taking the above summary of the project and organizational goals into consideration, here are some themes from which to develop your questions in Matrix Format.

Theme	Issues/Goals	Develop Questions to Target These Areas
Training	• New skill sets • Basic literacy • Computer literacy • Grant availability • Internal training resources • External training resources	• Specific skills needed • Current basic literacy levels • Current computer literacy levels • Grant resources • Current training resources available
Labor issues	• Job classifications • Pay structures • Testing • Selection process • Job elimination • Job combinations • Union's division of labor	• Past practices of selection and testing procedures • Union's contract language for these changes • Union's past participation level for similar changes • Impact of "pay for skills"

From your basic summary information you can build your assessment. The following pages will offer a wide range of possible questions to include.

NEEDS ASSESSMENT—SAMPLE QUESTIONS/FORM

Date _____

Contact: _____ Phone: _____

Email address _____

Technological Change (Equipment/Process/Improvement)

(Project Team Members)

Is the equipment/process/improvement new to the facility? _____

If so, what is the start-up date? _____

What will be new? _____

If not new, where (and when) else has it been installed/implemented?

_____

Who is familiar with it who could be useful as a resource?

_____

People (Operations/Maintenance/QC)

Number of people to be trained _____

Will any unions be affected by the changes? Which ones? How?

_____

Are employees allowed to train on shifts other than their own? _____

The number of trainees by group and shift:

Group	1st Shift	2nd Shift	3rd Shift
Operators			
Mechanics			
Electricians			
Electronic Technicians			
Stationary Engineers			
Supervisors			
Quality Personnel			
Others:			

- Are the employees all able to understand English? _____
  If not, what language/s? _____
  Give an estimate of the percentage of those who are non-English speaking _____

- What is the approximate maximum number of employees that could train at one time? By group?
  Operators_____ Mechanics_____ Electricians_____
  PL&H _____ ETs_____ QC_____
  Other_____

Equipment (Project Team)

Describe what *new* equipment/process will be installed, the vendor's name, and what new skills will be required by each.

Equipment/Process	Vendor	Skill Sets Required
Example: Case Packer	XYZ Manufacturer	Basic machine operation from a panel view screen. ABC programming language (for tech staff) PLC 500 Series (tech)
Case Sealer	BEA Manufacturer	(same as above)
Wrapper	Totte Manufacturer	Basic machine operation from a panel view screen Ability to read and interpret a troubleshooting guide—min. 6th-grade reading level

Once you've identified the skill sets required—column 3—you can develop another matrix, listing those skills in column 1 of the new matrix; follow that with a rating scale similar to page 80 to identify current skill levels. This will help you to find the skill "gaps."

Training Resources (HR/Operations/Maintenance)

- Do you currently have internal trainers?
  If so, list what type (maintenance, production, etc.) and how many (by shift).

- Do you have a train-the-trainer course?
  If so, who conducts it?

- Describe what training facilities are currently available.
  If none, where would you conduct the training?

- Check off what training aids you have available.
  _____ Flip charts _____ Overhead projector
  _____ Video player_____ Data projector
  _____ PLC simulators _____Computer lab
  List any others:

- Do you have a technical documentation library? _____
  If not, where is documentation kept?

- Do you have an apprenticeship program? If so, describe it.

- Do you have any training grants? Have you ever had any? If so, please describe.

- What will be done over the long term to measure, maintain, and improve operator SKAs (skills, knowledge, abilities)?

Training Materials Required (Operations/Maintenance)

Check what types of training materials you would like/need:

_____ Installation manual

_____ Maintenance manual/Job aids

_____Electrical _____Mechanical _____HVAC

_____ Operator manual

_____ Job aids

_____ Troubleshooting guides

_____ Other_____

Documentation should include:

_____ Systems overview

_____ Installation procedures

_____ Safety

_____ Tools and equipment

_____ Quality parameters

_____ Process flow

_____ Operating procedures

_____ Lubrication

_____ Cleaning procedures

_____ Troubleshooting guides

_____ Spare parts list and drawings

_____ Other_____

- What type of training materials currently work well for you?

Budget (Project Team)

- What budgetary resources are available?

Training Gaps (Operations/Maintenance/QC)

Thinking about the skill levels of each group below, estimate where their skills are now, in relationship to where they need to be to operate/implement the new equipment/process efficiently.

Use these comments as a guideline:

U = Uncertain

1 = Low skill level—need to start from the basics, little to no prior experience, capability, or training

3 = Good basic skill level, need only the specifics of the new equipment

5 = High skill levels, very little training is needed, have worked with very similar equipment effectively

Operators	U	1	2	3	4	5
Mechanics	U	1	2	3	4	5
Electricians	U	1	2	3	4	5
Electronic Technicians	U	1	2	3	4	5
Stationery Engineers	U	1	2	3	4	5
Supervisors	U	1	2	3	4	5
Quality Personnel	U	1	2	3	4	5
Others	U	1	2	3	4	5

- What would you say will be the biggest skill gaps?

- Can you think of any pretraining that may be needed?
  (I.e., basic literacy skills, like reading, or math, keyboarding, etc.)

- What would you estimate the literacy level of the location is for operators?

  _____ Maintenance staff_____ Operators (Has it been measured?)

Unions (Human Resources)

- How will the changes affect the union employees?

- Are there any contractual issues involved? Describe them.

- Who will work with the union to explain the changes? How will it be presented?

Cultural Changes (Ops/Maintenance/HR/QC)

- Along with the technical changes, will there be any cultural changes? (I.e., Changing to a team-based structure, self-directed work team, etc.) Describe them.

- How will these changes positively affect the union employees?

- How do you think these changes will be accepted? Why? Why not?

- What would need to happen to gain support and ownership for the changes?

- Think of a time in the past when a change was successfully introduced. What made it successful?

IDENTIFYING TRAINING BEST PRACTICES

(Ask all groups.)

- Think of a past project that had effective training. What made it effective? Why?

- What type of training documentation has been most effective in the past? (Describe.) Who prepared it? (I.e., manuals, pictures, checklists, procedures on the equipment)

- What would you like the outcome from this training initiative to be?

- What are your concerns? Questions?

CUSTOMIZATION

The sample questions just listed are both general and specific questions. Pick any that are appropriate for your project, or create your own. You should customize your questions based on the *project* and *organizational goals* you described. Some additional sample questions by department might be:

Safety

- How will the technological changes affect safety?
- Is there a plan to work with those new issues?
- Are there any particular safety practices that need to be reinforced with training during this project?
- What are the top safety concerns?
- What are your safety indicators? How are they measured? (Lost time accidents (LTA), severity rates, Worker's Comp cost, etc.)
- What kind of safety training currently exists? Who does it?
- What are the strengths of your current safety program? How can you build on those?
- What role do the end users play in safety? (Train, audit, etc.) Will this project change that?
- What HR/safety concerns could have an effect—positively or negatively—on the training for the new facility/process/equipment?

Quality

- What quality responsibilities do the end users of this project have? (I.e., QC checks, holds, testing)
- What quality responsibilities will change?
- How will that affect the end users?
- What type of training or new skills do you think you will need to support this project?
- Is there a training process that will be implemented?
- Who trains quality procedures? How? When?
- What are the strengths of your current quality program/dept.? How can you build on those?

NEEDS ASSESSMENT—SAMPLE SHORT FORM

Short Interview and/or Focus Group Format

Name_____ Date_____

Phone_____ Email Address_____

1. Describe to me what the goals of this project are. How does this support the overall organizational needs/goals? (You want to identify the project and organizational needs up front. These will become the targets for your recommendations/solutions.)

2. How do you think you can contribute the most to the success of the project? What is your role? (This will help you focus on that person's needs, as well as skills and interests, and help to build buy-in and partnership.)

3. What will be different because of this project, from both a technological and a people side? (You need to know both, since they are integrated.)

4. What skill gaps do you think exist?

5. What is needed to fill these skill gaps?

6. What are the strengths of the people/organization that will make this a successful project? Areas of opportunity?

7. Describe training from projects in the past that were successful. What type of training was used? What made it successful?

8. What type of training documentation has been most effective in the past? (Describe.) Who prepared it? (I.e., manuals, pictures, checklists, procedures on the equipment)

9. If you could design the ideal training for this project, what would it look like?

10. What makes you optimistic about the project? What are your concerns? Questions?

Thank you for your time and insights! The results will be sent to you by.....

LESSONS LEARNED

• Know *why* you are doing the needs assessment (project and organizational goals) and customize your questions to target those goals. *Don't* use generic formats that may not get what you need. Be efficient.

- If you hire an educational institution to do this, be aware of the time delay in getting it completed. They will be very thorough, but it may take longer and be more expensive than you want.

- Use a combination of techniques for the best results.

- *Always* show appreciation for people's participation and *share the results* in easy-to-understand terms. This will bring a lot of goodwill and support for your project. It will set the stage for them to participate again the next time! You're building a partnership here! Offering small incentives helps too—bookmark, pen, etc.)

APPRECIATIVE INQUIRY APPLICATION

? *Chapter 5—Needs Assessment*

In Chapter 5 we discussed:
- How, why, and when to do a needs assessment.
- The importance of identifying the project goals and how they fulfill an organizational need. How to design questions around them.
- Who should conduct and complete a needs assessment.
- The different assessment techniques.
- Sample questions that can be used.
- The importance of including the end users.

How was Appreciative Inquiry applied?
The person who develops the needs assessment questions needs to include questions that identify what works (the best of *what is*) as well as what the perceived strengths of the project team and organization are. These AI questions need to be asked to *all* who participate. Some of these questions might include:

- What are the strengths of the people/organization that will make this a successful project? (Best of *what is*.)
- How do you think you can contribute the most to the success of the project? What is your role?
- Describe the training from a project in the past that was successful. What kind of training was used that accomplished the project goals? What made it successful? (Best of *what is*.)

- What from that experience do you think we could apply to this project? (What *could be*.)
- If you could design the ideal training for this project, what would it look like? (What *could be*.)
- Who do you notice always helping/coaching/training others? Who do you put new employees with to learn? (Best of *what is*.)
- What internal resources do you have that could have a very positive impact on the results of the project? (Best of *what is*.)
- What about the project will make the people supportive?
- What type of training documentation has been most effective in the past? (Describe.) Who prepared it? (Best of *what is*.)

  (I.e., manuals, pictures, checklists, procedures on the equipment)
- What makes people optimistic about the project?

Take all the *best of* comments, discuss energetically what *could be* then develop what *will be*. This is the core of your successful training plan, built on a positive appreciative foundation.

QUESTIONS TO ASK ABOUT NEEDS ASSESSMENTS

- Who, internally, could develop and conduct the needs assessment process?
- If no one, who externally could do it?
- What are the goals of the project, and how do they support the organizational needs/goals?
- Who should participate in the assessment, remembering that diversity of opinion is important, as well as the full range of those affected by the project? How many?
- How much time will this process take?
- When should/can we complete this assessment?
- How do we do it efficiently and cost-effectively?
- Who will tally the results? Present them? To whom?
- How will the results be distributed to the participants?
- How do we get buy-in to support this process?
- Will an MTM study be done (motion time management) to support your recommendations to the union?

6

Developing Your Internal Resources

Productive things don't happen on a project without planning and a good, solid coordination of efforts. The training for projects is no exception.

Two of the most important roles for the *people side* of project management are the *training coordinator* and the *trainers*—both internal and external. The following pages will review roles, responsibilities, and the selection process.

TRAINING COORDINATOR

Typically, the technical project team members are far too busy coordinating with contractors and vendors, as well as other project members, to do justice to the coordination of the training. It's a good idea to select someone that has a stake in the success of the project, and also has a sincere interest in effective training, to coordinate the training efforts. This person may be the same one who developed and conducted the needs assessment, or someone with similar traits (refer to Chapter 5). Critical traits that must be added to the list are *patience* and *flexibility*. Inevitably, every plan this person makes will be changed many times. It may even be good to have someone external, if appropriate. This is not a full-time position, but during the initial planning stage, then prior to and during installation and start-up, it may consume a substantial amount of time, depending on the size of the project. It is an excellent developmental role for an internal person.

Here is a general overview of the role, along with specific responsibilities that may be included. Of course, these will vary for each project and each company.

Role Overview—Training Coordinator

The training coordinator is responsible for the coordination of all training activities associated with the project, including, but not limited to: needs assessment, vendor contact, development of training objectives, format, evaluation, budgeting, and scheduling.

Responsibilities

- Contact vendors to identify/assess their capabilities to provide effective training—documentation, availability, trainers, evaluation process, and their overall training resources.
- Provide recommendations to fill any gaps that exist between what they can provide and what is needed. Find additional resources, if needed.
- Coordinate external and internal training resources—people and materials.
- Request training proposals from vendors. (Sample letter on page 96)
- Develop a training budget—labor, materials, and vendor costs.
- Work with project team members to clarify training provided for in the vendor's contracts, budgets (local and capitol), and CAR.
- Provide details of training needs to vendors.
- Schedule all training. (Sample schedules on pages 101–102)
- Communicate and develop training schedules in a timely manner.
- Develop training grant proposals and administer them. (This may fall out of the scope of this role—it may reside with HR or Accounting.)
- Coordinate all sign-in sheets, evaluations of instructors, and skill evaluations (performance checks of participants).
- Coordinate the logistics of the training.
- Perform assignments, as needed. (I.e., prepare copies of training materials, complete and submit grant paperwork.)

This can be a very rewarding job because you are helping to reduce the overall cost of the project when effective training is conducted ... however, it can be very frustrating at times when plans are cancelled, vendors don't show up when promised, or the trainees all of a sudden aren't available. The vendors must be held accountable for the training, but you *must* help that process a great deal. Remember that vendors are usually not in the training business. They are doing it because they have to. Keep in mind is that you both have the same goal—successful project results. Reinforce that continuously!

Building partnerships up front where expectations are known and accepted is *key*. Refer back to the case study in Chapter 1, which elaborates on an effective process for doing that.

Things You Can Do to Help the Training Process

✔ Know what you want *before* you talk to vendors about training. Develop your own training specs, and give them a copy. This helps them tremendously and enhances the possibility of your getting what you need.

✔ Be flexible with them. Look at what they have in the way of training materials and instructors, and go from there. Offer suggestions to fill in the gaps you see. If you expect your specs to be met exactly, also expect to *pay* for it and *wait* for it.

✔ Talk to the vendor trainers prior to the training so you are sure that they understand your expectations. If you aren't comfortable with their trainer, ask for a different one. Make sure that the vendor trainer is there to train. Frequently, a vendor sends a service rep to install and *if* there is time, to train. It's difficult to do both, and it's always the training that suffers.

✔ Always get a copy of their training outline/process and how they will evaluate whether or not learning has occurred. This is something they don't like to deal with because no one has probably ever asked them to do that. Make it realistic. Develop performance checks with them. (Sample in Chapter 7.)

TOOLS FOR THE COORDINATOR

The training coordinator will need a few tools to help the process along. Some of the most useful ones are:

• Letters to the vendors—introduction, proposal, and training requirements

- Training specs (Chapter 7)
- Training schedules (Chapter 6)
- Performance checks (Chapter 7)

Letters to the Vendors

- Letter of introduction (Chapter 2)
- Letter of training requirements (Chapter 6)
- Request for information and proposal (Chapter 6)

Letter to Vendor—Project Training Requirements

Dear Vendor,

Subject: Project XYZ-Project Training Requirements
In preparation for the upcoming training for Project XYZ, I am sending:

- The specific training content needed for each group
- Number of trainees, by group and shift
- Number that can be released for training at one time
- Materials required
- The training windows we have to support the project properly

Once you review this information and your resources available, we can begin to identify a specific schedule to be implemented.

Job Title	*Number of people to be trained.* *(Number that can be released at one time)*
Training Content:	
Materials Required:	
Training Window:	

Knowing that each group may require a different instructor, I'm sending this information to you early so that we can secure their availability for these dates. We would also be happy to have one or two of each group train at your site prior to the in-house training. These individuals (internal trainers) could then assist you while you are training at our location.

I will call you next Wednesday to discuss the details of this scheduling. Feel free to contact me sooner at 333-444-5678.

Sincerely,

Susan Sunday
Training Coordinator
333-444-4455
333-444-4459 (fax)
sundays@hht.com

Letter to Vendor—Training Requirements—Completed Sample
Dear Vendor,

Subject: Project XYZ—Project Training Requirements
In preparation for the upcoming training for Project XYZ, I am sending:

- The specific training content needed by each group
- Number of trainees, by group and shift
- Number of trainees that can be released at one time (italicized)
- Materials required
- The training windows we have to support the project properly

Once you review this information and your resources available, we can begin to identify a specific schedule to be implemented.

Operators	*8 per shift (24 total)*	*8 per shift*
Supervisors	*2 per shift (6 total)*	*1 per shift*

Training Content:
- Overview of the equipment/process/system
- Safety
- Parts and their function
- Operating procedures

- Controls (Man Machine Interface—MMI)
- Troubleshooting
- Cleaning procedures

Materials Required: Manuals, job aids (troubleshooting guide, critical operating procedures)

Training Window: January 15–30—1st shift

February 15–30—2nd Shift

March 1–15—3rd shift

Mechanics	*4 per shift (12 total) 2–3 per shift*
	We could overlap shifts.

Training Content:

- Overview of the equipment/process/system
- Safety
- Installation procedures
- Machine-operating procedures
- Controls (Man Machine Interface—MMI)
- Preventive maintenance procedures and lubrication
- Repair and replacement procedures
- Troubleshooting/diagnostic procedures
- Cleaning procedures

Materials Required: Manuals, job aids (troubleshooting guide, lubrication index, changeover procedures, PM schedule, parts list)

Training Window: January 7–25—1st shift

February 1–10—2nd Shift (**Shifts may be combined)**

February 1–10—3rd shift

Electricians, Electronic Techs (E.T.), Engineers	*3 per shift (9), 2 per shift (6), 2 total We can overlap shifts to allow 3 electricians and E.T.'s in each session. One engineer can be released.*

Training Content:

- Overview of the equipment/process/system

- Safety

- Electrical/electronic calibration and testing

- Electrical/electronic troubleshooting

- Man Machine Interface (MMI)

- PLC and controls architecture and strategy

- PLC and controls calibration, testing, and troubleshooting

- Repair and replacement procedures

- Programming (ETs and engineers only)

- Robotics theory and design (if appropriate)

- Robotics calibration, testing, and troubleshooting

- Robotics repair and replacement

Materials Required: Manuals, job aids, schematics, with electronic media

Training Window: January 7–25—1st shift
February 1–10—2nd Shift (**Shifts may be combined.**)
February 1–10—3rd shift

Knowing that each group may require a different instructor, I'm sending this information to you early so that we can secure their availability for these dates. We would also be happy to have one or two of each group train at your site prior to the in-house training. These individuals (internal trainers) could assist you while you are training at our location.

I will call you next Wednesday to discuss the details of this scheduling. Feel free to contact me sooner at 333-444-5678.

Sincerely,

Susan Sunday
Training Coordinator
333-444-4455
333-444-4459 (fax)
sundays@hht.com

Letter Requesting Information and Proposal

Dear........,

Now that we know what training resources you have (from the initial training questionnaire from Chapter 2), I am sending you our specific training needs from which we'd like you to develop a proposal for the total training cost. I also would like you to send me:

- The training time you need for each group
- The maximum number of trainees you can accommodate in each group
- Training outlines for each group

You'll also want to review the training specs that we discussed earlier in the project. (Copy attached)

Group of Employees	Time Needed to Train	Maximum Trainees per Group
Operators		
Mechanics		
Electricians		
Electronics Technicians		
Engineers		
HVAC		
Others		

Along with this information, can any of these groups be combined for some or all of the training? I will follow up on (date) to discuss this information, but you can also fax it to me at............ With this information I can begin to develop a schedule to work out with you.

Here is another format:

Dear Vendor,

Now that we know what training resources you have, we'd like you to prepare a training proposal from our specific training needs, listed below. We are now looking at conducting the training early in January through February. If you need any additional information, please don't hesitate to contact me.

Thanks for your help on this project.

Listed below is information to utilize to help you develop a training proposal for us.

Type	Number to be trained	Number that can be taken off the line for training at one time
Operators		
Mechanics		
Electricians		
Electronics Technicians		
Supervisors		
Stationary Engineers		

All training will be done on 1st shift.

Information we'd like in the training materials

Training Content Matrix *Topics that should be included in each type of employee training.*							
Topic	*Operator*	*Mechanic*	*Electrician*	*Electronics Technician*	*Stationary Engineer*	*Supervisor*	
System/Equipment Overview							
Safety							
Tools & Parts							
Installation							
Start-Up							
Operating Procedures							
Shut Down							
Troubleshooting							
Repair & Maintenance							
Electrical Schematics							

Type of training materials we'd like
Manual that include:

- _____ Installation procedures (not for training)
- _____ Safety
- _____ Operating procedures
- _____ Troubleshooting guides
- _____ Maintenance procedures
- _____ Preventive Maintenance (PMs)

- _____ Parts list

- _____ Other (describe)

Job Performance Aids (JPAs)

- _____ Checklists

- _____ Troubleshooting guides

- _____ Specific procedures

- _____ Diagrams

- _____ Evaluation performance checks   H = Helpful, if available

Sample—Completed Letter Requesting Proposal

Listed below is information to utilize to help you develop a training proposal for us.

Type	Number to be trained	Number that can be taken off theline for training at one time
Operators	7	3–4
Mechanics	9	4–5
Electricians	5	2–3
Electronics Technicians		
Supervisors	5	Will be in operators group
Stationary Engineers		

All training will be done on 1st shift.

Information we'd like in the training materials

Training Content Matrix _Topics that should be included in each type of employee training._							
Topic	_Operator_	_Mechanic_	_Electrician_	_Electronics Technician_	_Stationary Engineer_	_Supervisor_	
System/Equipment Overview	X	X	X			X	
Safety	X	X	X			X	
Tools & Parts	X	X	X			X	
Installation							
Start-Up	X	X	X			X	
Operating Procedures	X	X	X			X	
Shut Down	X	X	X			X	
Troubleshooting	X	X	X			X	
Repair & Maintenance		X	X			X	
Electrical Schematics			X				

Type of training materials we'd like
Manuals that include:

- __X__ Installation procedures (not for training)
- __X__ Safety
- __X__ Operating procedures
- __X__ Troubleshooting guides
- __X__ Maintenance procedures
- __X__ Preventive Maintenance (PMs)
- __X__ Parts list
- _____ Other (describe)

Job Performance Aids (JPAs)

- __H__ Checklists
- __X__ Troubleshooting guides
- _____ Specific procedures
- __X__ Diagrams
- __H__ Evaluation performance checks   H = Helpful, if available

TRAINING SCHEDULES

 Once you have gotten all the specifics, you can develop a detailed schedule. It should be easy to read and contain all the important information—time, place, instructor, and group. This should be communicated to all parties involved and the logistics confirmed. *Always have a backup in mind.* Remember that a big percentage of this training will be on-line or in a lab once the general information is discussed in the primary classroom.

Sample (Weekly Schedule)

Week of January 15—1st Shift					
		Operators	*Mechanics*	*Electrician/ ET/Eng*	*HVAC*
Monday	AM				
	PM	Systems Overview—All Groups			
Tuesday	AM	Group 1		Group 1	
	PM	Group 2			
Wednesday	AM		Group 1	Group 1 On-line	On-line Group 1
	PM		Group 2		On-line Group 2
Thursday	AM	Group 1		Group 2	
	PM	Group 2			
Friday	AM	Group 1 On-line		Group 2 On-line	
	PM	Group 2	On-line		

The *weekly schedule* gives a good overview of who will be in training and what day it will take place. It could also list names for each group.

The *daily schedule* gives much more detail: rooms, instructors, and times. Both are important and should be sent out together. If it's a large project, it's good to have a *shared folder* on the computer set up for anyone to check this information and any other project information. These schedules are subject to change, so you must constantly keep them updated. Make sure each update contains a revision date and time on it, to help eliminate confusion.

Sample (Daily Schedule)

	Operators Supervisors	Mechanics	Electricians Ets/Engrs.	HVAC
	January 15—1st Shift			
7:30– 9:30 AM	Basic Equipment Overivew—All Groups Classroom A Instructor—John			
9:45– 11:30	Basic Operations Classroom A Instructor—Sally Group #1		Electronic Systems Overview Group 1 Classroom B Instructor—Jack	
12:15– 3:00	On-Line Group 1 Training Instructor—Sally		Programming Technical Lab 1 Instructor—Jack	

INTERNAL TRAINERS

One of the most effective ways to develop your internal capabilities is to select and train internal trainers. It's a developmental opportunity for your staff and creates an ongoing learning environment. Equally important, you reduce your dependence on external resources, saving money and time. Not only is this cost-effective; it makes overall good business sense.

A few things to consider when doing this are:

- Appropriateness for your needs
- Selection criterion and process
- Special classification and pay issues
- Union considerations

Appropriateness for Your Needs

Having trainers is most appropriate when you will be doing repeat training over a period of time, with many people. If there is a short period of training for a highly technical skill needed, and only a few people to be trained, it's more cost-effective to hire an external resource. By the time you'd train someone to the skill level needed, it would probably be too late, and that person still wouldn't have the same ability to be considered a subject matter expert (SME). If a skill is highly technical and probably has a short life span, it's also better to use the external resource.

Select and Train Internal Trainers When:

✔ The skill to be taught will be used by many people over a period of time.

✔ Many people will need to be trained and/or retrained on the skill.

✔ There are internal people (SMEs) who possess or can easily be trained on the skills needed because of comparable skills they possess.

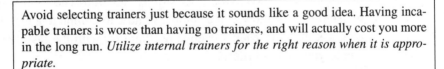

Avoid selecting trainers just because it sounds like a good idea. Having incapable trainers is worse than having no trainers, and will actually cost you more in the long run. *Utilize internal trainers for the right reason when it is appropriate.*

Selecting Trainers

There are several basic criteria that are critical in the selection of trainers (and/or facilitators). Along with those, you must also decide what's important to you and add those criteria to your list.

The key selection components for internal trainers are:

- Expertise and/or job classification
- Communication skills
- General positive traits of an employee

Expertise

When asked "what makes good trainers?" the answer most often heard is *that the people know what they are talking about and doing*. They must have a good *working* knowledge of the subject matter and application of it. If your project is bringing in new technology that perhaps hasn't been used before, then the people must have the basic theory and understanding of comparable systems/equipment/processes so that they could easily learn the new information and application of it. I'll call these "technical basics." ("Technical" here refers to *any* subject matter, whether it be listening skills or troubleshooting a piece of equipment.) In some cases, you may need specific educational requirements, but usually in the workplace experience is far more important.

Therefore, you should put on your list of selection criteria specific knowledge and application parameters, such as:

- One to two years' experience on PLC controls
- Two years of computer systems troubleshooting experience

Communication Skills

Along with good "working" technical skills, the ability to communicate them is absolutely essential. We all remember the barriers that were created for our own learning when instructors just couldn't get their points across. When selecting a trainer, it's mandatory that the potential trainers *demonstrate* their communication skills in a learning situation. The ideal way to do that is to ask that they show you a sample of how to complete a technical task, and then ask them to teach someone not familiar with the task how to do it. So add to your list of criteria:

- Good communication skills and the ability to demonstrate them

General Positive Traits of an Employee

You don't want people who have poor work records, even though they may be good communicators with solid technical skills, to be your trainers. It would send the wrong message and cause conflict. It's important to use criteria that are not subjective, and don't violate either governmental or union rules.

The one that stands out here is attendance. ADA (Americans with Disability Act) prohibits discrimination based on disabilities. People's disabilities may cause them to miss work frequently, so their attendance records may appear poor. You can't penalize a person for a disability, but if travel to a vendor's location or continuous training for a period of time is a *bona fide* requirement, then you're okay to add this to your list of selection criteria if their disability would inhibit them from both, and if these are primary responsibilities. Here are some sample criteria you *might* add under this category: Again, you need to define what's important to you. I caution you to be sensitive to both governmental regulations/laws and union contractual agreements.

- Must be in good employment standings (those on probation will not be considered, nor will those with significant work problems in the past year. You need to define *significant* clearly.)
- Must be able to travel out of town, when needed.
- Must have a good attendance record. (No one on attendance probation will be considered.)
- Must be able to read, write, and speak in English (if appropriate).

Those are the basics; you add what's important to your situation.

The Process

A selection process that has worked well is as follows:

- Identify your selection criteria.
- Review that with Human Resources and union leadership via or with HR.
- Develop a posting and adhere to your normal posting procedures, but make sure it is clear that this is *not* a full-time job (if it's not). Have the selection process clearly stated, and if needed, hold an informational session. If this is new, a short session is very helpful and allows for questions and clarifications.
- Collect names and applications, if used. (If it's hourly employees, you'll probably just collect their names/clock numbers from the posting, not an application.)

- Review employees' qualifications for the basic requirements.
- Notify those who don't qualify that they were eliminated, and why, and schedule interviews for the others. (Use an interview team of HR and SMEs.)
- Conduct interviews, demonstrations, and supervisor's references.
- Select trainers based on scores and references.

Caution!

Make sure that you have cleared the selection criteria with your Human Resources Department to ensure that you are not discriminating or violating any governmental or negotiated regulations!

Sample Posting

Posting Dates: 10/15/02–10/30/02

Controls Trainer Position

We are actively seeking a CONTROLS TRAINER to support the training for Project XYZ. This position is *not* a full-time position but will be needed during the period of January 1–April 15, and from then, on an "as needed" basis. All who are interested must meet these requirement and sign the posting no later than October 30, 2002.

Basic Requirements:
- Must be in good employment standing.
  (Anyone on probation will not be eligible.)
- Must be available during January 1–April 15.
- Must be able to attend off-site seminars, when needed.
- Must be flexible to work on both 1st and 2nd shift, as needed.
- Must be able to read, write, and speak in English.

Technical Requirements:
- Must have one to two years' experience working on Controls systems and being in the current classification of Electronic Technician (ET).
- Must be able to replace, repair, and troubleshoot systems.
- Must have good communication skills, especially the ability to communicate information to trainees—verbally and through demonstrations.

Candidates that meet these requirements will participate in the following selection process: (To be conducted 11/15–11/30.)

- A verbal interview
- A demonstration of your ability to do a technical task
- A demonstration of your ability to teach someone else that task.

Sign Up

Name	Clock Number	Current Position	Current Shift

If you have any questions, contact......

Sample—Trainer Candidate Evaluation

Control Trainer—Evaluation Form

Section 1: The interview			
	Rating		
Questions	1—Poor	2—Good	3—Excellent
1. Why do you want to be a trainer?			
2. Describe a time when you were at your best as a coach, Sunday school teacher, facilitator, trainer or teacher—formally or informally.			

	Rating		
Questions	*1—Poor*	*2—Good*	*3—Excellent*
3. Describe the traits of the best trainer/teacher you've ever seen or had. Now, rate yourself on each of those traits on a scale of 1–5, 5 being the best.			
4. Describe a safety problem in the facility that needs to be corrected. What could *you* do to get it corrected?			
5. Describe a difficult task that you had to learn in the past five years (here at work). What helped you learn it? If you had to teach it, how would you do that?			
6. What are the strengths of your department, and how do you contribute to them?			

You will also want to include technical questions here or in the next section.

Section 2: Demonstrate a task	Rating		
	1—Poor	2—Good	3—Excellent
(This is where you select a very specific task that will give you an idea of their technical knowledge. Pick a realistic and short task, and ask questions as they demonstrate. (Help them relax during the process.)			
Example: Demonstrate how you would change a chain on the xyz machine. (List the steps on this form so all evaluators are looking for the same thing). An example of steps might begin this way: A. Check that the machine is shut down and the power is off. B. Put the lockout tag on. C. Remove the screws from the guard. D. With a screwdriver, lift the chain off the teeth. Continue with steps..........			
Section 3: Teach someone to do the task you just demonstrated			
Watch the potential trainer for these elements.			
• Explains safety elements of the task first			
• Helps to relax the trainee before starting			
• Explains steps slowly, allowing for questions			
• Has good eye contact			
• Listens attentively			
• Allows the trainee to try the steps, with guidance			
• Asks questions of the trainee			

Section	Total Score of Section
Section 1: Questions	
Section 2: Demonstration of task	
Section 3: Trains that task	
Total Score:	

Reference from Supervisor:

____Excellent   ____Good   ____Poor

____Excellent, or good worker, but don't recommend for a trainer

Evaluators: _____ **Date:** _____

Selection Stories

Selection can be a *very sensitive* issue. Here are a few situations that you can learn from.

- At a manufacturing facility, we were going to introduce team-based lines for the very first time. In deciding on selection criteria for the team members, we considered how important their reading levels were. To make sure that we were legally requiring skills that were valid, we requested the assistance of the local community college. They conducted a job analysis and found that some basic math skills were required, but as far as reading skills, it was recognition that was important rather than a specific reading level. They then identified the appropriate tests that we could administer during the selection process. You can't assume reading and math levels—you need to be sure, or don't test.

- Testing is a very hot issue when unions are involved, so we worked extensively with our labor relations manager and got the union to understand and accept our need for testing. Those that met our initial requirements (good work and attendance record) then took the tests. What a surprise at the levels! And what a reaction employees had. One mother and daughter took the test, and only the daughter passed. It caused quite a bit of dissension between them. And one gentleman who didn't pass brought in his high school math papers to show that he could do it. So if you plan to test, be prepared. One thing that helped ease the fear at another location was a practice test. We made a short test available prior to the selection process, graded it, and gave them recommendations on what to brush up on. This helped tremendously!

LESSONS LEARNED

- Be absolutely sure that what you request in the trainer selection process is needed; otherwise, you open yourself up for problems.
- Don't use tests unless you can validate that the skills are needed.
- The word "test" is often frightening, especially to hourly employees who may not have high literacy levels. Avoid the word if possible. Use "evaluation" or "performance check" instead.
- If you do use a formal test, make a sample available before the selection process begins so people can prepare or have a better idea of what is expected. Provide learning resources to improve their skills whenever possible. (I.e., names of schools that offer free Adult Basic Education or English as a Second Language classes.)
- *Be consistent* in the selection process.
- Make sure that HR has been a part of the process.
- Make the process realistic for your needs—not time-consuming.

THE BEST OF *WHAT IS*

Selecting and training internal trainers is one of the most effective things that you can do to build your companies' capacities! You are identifying the best of your resources and giving them the opportunity to grow and develop not only themselves but also others.

The benefits grow exponentially as they do the following:

Internal Trainers:

- Take pride and ownership in what they do.
- Become leaders not only in training but often become resources for equipment/process selection, change management, and problem resolution.
- Become empowered and involved in the business, not just the job. They become company ambassadors.
- Become role models for others.
- Take some of the load off of the supervisors and managers, partnering with them.

- Give you their best and more.

- Personally take more responsibility for their own professional growth, wanting to improve their skills versus waiting for it to happen to them.

- Their self-esteem grows as they see what they are capable of.

- Speak the same language as their trainees and understand their issues and concerns, making them more impactful in how they train.

You may ask why you don't just pick the person who you think will be a good trainer rather than go through this process. The answer is that you can, and you probably will at times. But going through an open selection process creates so many more opportunities to tap into *hidden talent*. It offers new possibilities to people who didn't have access to them before. You'll be pleasantly surprised by the potential that is unleashed when employees become trainers. They not only become trainers, but leaders. Too often we always go to the same people for everything—this way we tap new resources instead.

UNION CONSIDERATIONS

Unions exist to protect the best interests of the employees, with negotiated contracts that serve as their guide. Your job, as management, is to understand and abide by the contract you've both agreed to, and to have open and informational discussions about any changes that are needed. Labor and management should work as *partners* because they are. They both are looking out for the best interests of the company and its employees. Here are a few items that you need to consider when selecting union hourly trainers so the process is a positive experience. (Many of these items apply to nonunion environments too.)

All of these comments and suggestions may or may not be valid in your specific union, but they are issues that you need to understand.

- *Trainers' Classification*

  Usually, creating a new job classification is a negotiated item. But since this is most often not a full-time, permanent position, it can become a local agreement. If it becomes a local agreement, it should be written down and be administered consistently. (We had trainers within each classification and on each shift that were the trainers whenever training was needed.)

- *Trainers' Pay*

  Many times, trainers will receive additional pay, but *only* when they are training. This sounds logical, but the problem occurs in defining what that means. Does it mean anytime they help out someone, or does it mean when they are *formally* training and only training. This is an area that could cause problems if not done consistently. Be very careful that you think this through.

- **Trainers' Selection**

  Although this has been covered, it needs to be reemphasized that you need to take time to define the selection criteria and the process well, and then administer it consistently. The selection team should consist of HR and SMEs. Everyone *must* get asked the same questions— no exceptions!

- **Seniority**

  Seniority is the golden rule within union contacts. I strongly suggest that seniority *not* be a selection criterion for trainers, except if there is a tie among the final candidates. It's so important that you have the *best* trainer, not just the person with the most seniority. This definitely has to be agreed to first and foremost with the union leadership. HR *must* be involved in this process!

- **Shift Assignment**

  Shift assignments are decided by seniority, but often during project training periods the trainers are needed to work on shifts other than their own. This usually is not in violation of a union contract, but you need to check that out with your union so you have that flexibility.

APPRECIATIVE INQUIRY APPLICATION

Chapter 6—Developing Your Internal Resources

In Chapter 6 We Discussed:
- Roles and responsibilities of the training coordinator and internal trainers
- Tools for the coordinator
- Appropriateness for internal trainers
- Selection criteria and process for trainers
- Union considerations about internal trainers

How Was and Can Appreciative Inquiry Be Applied?
- ✔ The main example of the use of AI questioning was in the interview process, with these questions:

- Describe the strength of your department and how you contribute to that.
- Describe a time when you saw a safety problem, and what positive actions you took to resolve it. What safety actions have the greatest effect? How could we use more of them (what *could be*)?
- Describe a time when you demonstrated the traits of a good trainer. (Best of *what is*.)

✔ Also, when you are doing the *reference checks* on potential trainers, ask:

- Describe to me a time that they demonstrated the traits of a good trainer.

When thinking of the benefits of trainers, ask yourself what is the best of *what is* and what *could and will be* with the people you have. Work from past positive experiences rather than dwelling on the negative.

✔ When working with the unions, discussing the trainers' selection process and general guidelines, ask them AI questions, like:

- Can you think of a time when our current employees took on the role of trainers and how it created positive results? Describe it. (Best of *what is*.)
- Thinking about the traits that made those individuals such good trainers, what comes to mind? How could we apply this again (what *could* and *will be*)?

This is an important thought process to follow to gain support for having the trainer be the *best* person for the job, not just the most senior.

Let me reemphasize that asking appreciative questions is just the first step. You then must "imagine" what *could* be (Step 2) and develop concrete, realistic steps for what *will* be (Step 3).

QUESTIONS TO ASK ABOUT DEVELOPING YOUR INTERNAL RESOURCES

Training Coordinator

- Do we need a training coordinator for this project? If so, how much time do you estimate that it will demand of them?
- Is there anyone on the project team who could do this effectively? Anyone who wants to do it?

- Should the person be internal or external?
- What traits does this person have to possess in order to be effective?
- What, specifically, do we want this person to do?

Internal Trainers

- Can this project reach its goals faster and more effectively with the use of internal trainers?
- Is enough training required to warrant the use of internal trainers?
- Do we have internal candidates with the skills required to become effective trainers?
- What qualities do we need and want in a trainer?
- What selection process will we use?
- Do we need approval, and if so, from whom?
- How will the unions respond to having trainers?
- Who would train the trainers once selected?

7

Documentation

Accurate and timely documentation for projects is one of those never-ending quests. Everyone needs it, everyone wants it, but until the project is debugged and tested repeatedly, it's hard to provide it as completely as required. Documentation is used to design, build, train, implement, and troubleshoot—it's an incredibly important component of any project. By using some of the ideas and formats in this section, you can begin to:

- Identify what training documentation you want and need
- Create your own specs format and content
- Ask you vendors for documentation more effectively
- Create your own documentation internally

Remember, we are only talking about the *people side of project documentation*, not the technical pieces. Here is the difference:

Documentation

Technical	People Side
• Floor plans/layouts	• Training documentation specs*
• Electrical diagrams	• Training manuals
• CAD drawings	• Job performance aids
• Equipment specification	• Diagrams

• P&ID's	• Troubleshooting guides*
• Schematics	• Job breakdowns*
• Machine drawings	• Critical operating procedures*
	• Checklists*
	• Performance checks*
	• Simulations
	• E-Learning
	• Expert systems

*These areas will be focused on, and samples provided.

TRAINING AND DOCUMENTATION SPECS

The old saying goes, "you won't get what you want unless you ask for it"—this absolutely applies to training and documentation. When projects time gets tight, rather than asking specifically for what we need, training becomes one of those assumed project components. Complaints brew when things don't go well, yet 95 percent of the time, when it comes to training, we don't really give vendors and trainers a clear understanding of our needs and expectations. A great way to eliminate that problem is to develop a set of *training and documentation specs* and include your vendors in the process.

One of the best examples to illustrate this was when we decided—for the very first time—to develop formal training and documentation specs. Because we were doing it for the entire division, it was quite an involved process. After much discussion with all those who would be affected—maintenance, engineering, operations, HR, purchasing—we invited our primary vendors from around the world to take a look at our recommendations. The purpose of the meeting was to introduce our specs and get their input and buy-in, since these guidelines would represent our new expectations. The meeting started with an overview of our company's goals and direction, and then went on to our training and documentation specs. (It was important that they saw and heard the big picture, so they understood the *why* behind what we were asking them.) We also explained how this could benefit them, giving their businesses a competitive edge. Their enthusiastic participation was overwhelming. One comment sums it up nicely. "Now that we know what you want we can provide it. No one has ever told us before, nor included us in the process." Many of them had the tools and capabilities, but just didn't know what we wanted. This approach is so basic, yet rarely done. It was a great lesson and led to a progressive partnering that brought significant improvements.

The process described here may be more than you need, but it will give you a sense of what's possible. The examples that follow will help you develop your own realistic specs, in a relatively quick manner.

Developing Your Training and Documentation Specs

Below, you'll find a list of options that you may want to include in your specs. Remember to develop guidelines that meet your needs appropriately—don't make them more elaborate than needed because they can become overwhelming to vendors. (When we were completing this process, the entire division had to be accurately represented, so our specs became a very detailed 35-page spiral book with a disk.) You may want and need that, or you may prefer a one-to-two-page document. Use this checklist as your starting point, and once you've identified *what* you want, by category, begin to fill in the specific details for each.

Training and Documentation Checklist

To Be Included	*Topic*
	Training Manual Format
	• Size/style (spiral bound, binder, side bound) • Font style/size • Photos • Graphics • Diagrams • Reproducible electronic copy format (disk, CD) • Reading level • Other
	Types of Training Manuals and Content
	• Operator • Mechanical • Electrical/Electronic • Installation • Trainer • Other For each type of manual, you'll need to list the specific content required.

To Be Included	Topic
	Instructor Expectations
	• Experience • References • Contact information • Evaluation/measurement procedures
	Job Performance Aids (JPAs)
	• Critical Operating Procedures (COPs) • Troubleshooting guide • Checklists (i.e., start-up/shutdown) • Changeover procedures • Job breakdowns • Performance checks • Overview and/or flow diagrams • Simulation exercises • Others
	Bid Content
	• Project scope • Cost breakdown • List and dates of deliverables (training, materials, etc.) • Scheduling • Contact information • Special needs

Now that you have a checklist to work from, here is a sample of the kind of specific information you might have in your own specs.

SAMPLE FORMAT

Training and Documentation Specs—XYZ Company

These training and document specs represent our expectations for all deliverables requested. Any exceptions to this must be discussed and approved by XYZ Company. Additions may be made at any time, as needed.

	Training Manual Format
Size	A 3-ring binder with labeled tabs, $8^1/_2 \times 11$, printed front and back. Each manual should have a table of contents, a labeled cover, and spine. (At times, a spiral book may be appropriate.)
Font style/size	Use Arial, Tahoma, or Times Roman font, no smaller than 12 point.
Photos	Only high-quality photos that can be reproduced on a laser color printer. All must be labeled with a title and number.
Graphics and illustrations	All must be labeled with a title and number.
Diagrams/drawings	These are to illustrate a piece of equipment, a product/process flow, or the steps of procedures. Always show an arrow to indicate the direction of the flow. Each should be titled and numbered and should be able to fit into a manual if folded. (List the engineering software program needed.)
Electronic copy	We require all electronic copies to be IBM compatible in the latest Microsoft WORD version. This is important so that we can update it independently. (List other software as required, like Excel, etc.) Provide copies on $3^1/_2$ disk and CD ROM.
Other information	
Reading level	The reading level of the operating manuals should *not* exceed eighth grade.
Reproducible copy	A reproducible hard copy should be submitted for all documentation. These will be unbound.
Graphic orientation	We prefer the manuals to be as graphic as possible—at least every 2 or 3 pages.

Types and Content of Training Manuals (You'll probably want a list of content for each job classification.)	
Operators' Manuals	• Systems/process overview • Safety • Parts, tools, and their functions • Start-up and shutdown procedures (also emergency ones) • Operating procedures (including controls) • Quality/product parameters • Troubleshooting • Sanitation procedures • Other
Mechanics' Manuals	• Systems/process overview • Safety • Setup, calibration, and timing • Lubrication • Troubleshooting • Spare parts lists and replacement (preventative maintenance) schedule • Repair and replacement procedures • Man Machine Interface (MMI)
Electricians' Electronics Technicians' Manuals	• Systems and electrical overview • Safety • Setup and calibration • Repair and replacement procedures • Man Machine Interface (MMI) • Troubleshooting • Spare parts and drawings

	• Schematics and wiring diagrams • Controls architecture • PLC codes
Instructors' Manual	• Training/learning objectives • Course outlines, times, teaching hints, materials needed • Evaluation procedures (including performance checks) • Handouts, overhead transparencies, disks • Reference materials • Certificates of Achievement

Job Performance Aids (JPAs)

Job Performance Aids are short guides to enhance learning and continued use of proper procedural steps. They are typically a specific task of a job, or a procedure for a piece of equipment or process. JPAs are often created for critical operating procedures (COPs).

Troubleshooting guide*	This should be in a small, laminated spiral-book format no larger than four by eight. It should be done in matrix format, which includes problem, possible causes, and possible solutions. Graphics and diagrams are very helpful, when appropriate.
Critical Operating Procedure (COP)	These should be laminated, one or two-page sheets, no larger than $8^{1}/_{2} \times 11$, preferably in color (if appropriate). There should always be a title of the procedure, steps should be numbered, and the flow of the process noted with an arrow.
Changeover Procedure	This is just a specialized form of a JPA, with the same guidelines as the COPs.
Checklist*	This includes the steps of a procedure and usually doesn't have graphics on it. (It may be a start-up procedure, for example.) The size will vary depending on the use, but typically this should be $8^{1}/_{2} \times 11$ and can be laminated or not, depending how it's being used.
Job breakdown*	This may be similar to the COP, but it is usually a learning tool that includes more detail and hints.

Equipment or process diagram	This is a visual guide to illustrate an entire piece of equipment and/or process. It should be well labeled and titled. This is usually on a larger-size paper, but should be able to fit into a manual if folded.
Performance Check* (PC)	A Performance Check is a trainers' tool used to identify whether trainees are able to perform the task they were trained on, or if additional training is needed. PCs have the steps of a process listed with a rating box after each. The bottom has a place for signatures confirming the trainee's ability to perform the task.

*Samples will be provided.

Instructors

To ensure that training is delivered effectively, we'd like the following information. It's important that the trainer is going to be dedicated to training and not trying to play a simultaneous role of installer and trainer.

Experience	Prefer at least two years' prior training. Provide a resume, if available.
References	Two references from prior training experience, and their phone numbers.
Contact information	Name, address, phone, cell phone, fax, email address.
Evaluation procedure	Samples will be requested.
Bid Request	
Project scope	A brief description of the project. This can be in narrative and/or bullet format.
Cost Details	These should be broken into three categories: • Time (labor hours) • Travel and expenses • Materials

Dates/schedules of deliverables	Schedules, availability, and deadlines should be included. For materials, deadlines for drafts and final copy should be included.
Contact	All contact information should be provided—name, address, phone, cell phone, fax, email address.
Your special needs	List any special needs *you* have in order to accomplish the agreed-upon training expectations; ex., training room, simulators, data projectors, overhead projector, etc.

The training and documentation specs provided to you are a guide to enhance your understanding of our training expectations. (Additional specs may be requested, as needed.) They should be applied while working on our training projects and should help avoid any misunderstandings. Just as we have shared these expectations with you, we welcome your questions, concerns, and recommendations.

As in any good partnership, we encourage you to let us know what your expectations of us are so that you can receive the support you need to provide the requested deliverables on time and within budget. We will be flexible as needed.

We look forward to a productive working partnership.
Feel free to contact me at:

Susan B. Sunshire   333-444-5566
Mr. Training and Development   333-444-5567 (fax)
XYZ Corporation   333-444-7908 (cell)
3350 Frizzle Road   sunshires@xyz.com
Dover, Delaware 66007

You could also put these specs in a matrix format as an overview as shown on the next page.

Training Documentation Specs Matrix

	Computer Platform	Size	Format	Contents
Manuals				
Operator's Manuals				
Mechanic's Manual				
Electrician's Manual				
Other Manuals				
Job Performance Aids				
Instructor's Guide				
Bid Content				
Electrical Diagrams and Schematics				
Graphics				

JOB PERFORMANCE AIDS (JPAs)

Job Performance Aids (JPAs) can be one of the most effective tools to assist people in learning and maintaining the new processes and/or equipment that your project is introducing. They really are anything that people use as aids to learning—JPAs can be checklists, process flow diagrams, simulators, job breakdown sheets, troubleshooting guides, etc. Some examples of JPAs that most of you have seen and used are: quick guides (one small piece of paper) for using your cordless or cell phones; the assembly diagram that came when you bought your computer showing, through the use of color coding and pictures, how to connect your computer to your printer and monitor; or the simple "cheat sheets" you made to remember critical steps for some tasks.

What makes JPAs so valuable is that they are quick and easy to use, and usually small. They can be carried conveniently in your pocket or in planners, or attached to a piece of equipment. Although manuals are valuable because of the needed details they contain, no one I know walks around with a manual in their hand, at least not for very long. Manuals serve a necessary purpose, but too often become dust collectors or get misplaced. When learning a new process you will start with a manual, but once your confidence increases, you'll move on to JPAs.

Benefits and Application

Manuals	Job Performance Aids
• Contain needed details, which are especially important during initial training and installation.	• Summarize a process in bullet format. • Particularly good for critical operating processes (COPs).
• Used as an ongoing resource and reference.	• Easy and quick to use.
• Used to verify processes.	• Small and handy (user-friendly).
• May be used by engineers and/or designers as a base from which to develop new prototypes.	• Can be very inexpensive to make. • Can be designed internally, quickly. • Can be updated easily and frequently.
• Usually provided by the supplier of the equipment/process.	• Can be used to help reduce cost and/or waste due to a recurring error.
• Provide critical information, especially safety contents, to fulfill a vendor's legal responsibilities.	• Do not replace detailed manuals, but are a supplement to them.

The next few pages will give you samples of some of the most basic Job Performance Aids that you can make internally, at very little cost. These can be used to design an entire training program or just as simple aids to help reduce cost and waste created by your top problem areas.

Job Breakdown

A *job breakdown* is a detailed list of steps it takes to complete a task. It includes not only the steps, but also the helpful hints that make it understandable to a new trainee.

Job Breakdown 1.0—How to Change a Flat Tire

Steps	Helpful Hints
Slow down and pull the car off the road.	Make sure it is all the way off and on a flat surface. Turn the engine off, put transmission in "P," and turn the emergency break and flashers on. Have everyone get out and away from traffic.
Park the car.	Put blocks under the tires to prevent rolling when it is jacked up. You can use any piece of wood or rocks as blocks. Blocks should be placed in front of the front tires and behind the back tires.
Get the spare tire, jack, and car wrench out of the trunk.	Check spare for air in it. If tire is low, get air at the nearest station once you drive off on the spare.
Loosen the wheel nuts before raising the car.	Turn the wrench counterclockwise to *loosen* nuts. Loosen opposite wheel nuts until they\ are all loosened. *Don't take them out yet!* To get maximum leverage, grab the wrench near the end of the handle, and pull up on the handle.

Position the jack under the car at the jack joints.	Make sure it is on a level and solid surface before jacking the car up. Make sure no one is in the car.
Jack the car up.	Insert the jack handle into the jack and turn clockwise. As it begins to lift, check again that it is properly positioned. *Never* get under the car supported by a jack. Make sure it is high enough so the spare can be installed.
Remove the wheel nuts and tire.	Once you take the nuts off, put them in the hubcap or another safe place. Lift tire off and put aside.
Put spare tire on.	Wipe off any corrosion on the mounting surface first so the nuts won't loosen up while driving. Align the wheel holes with the bolts, wiggle it on, and press it back.
Put the wheel nuts back on.	Tighten all the nuts as much as you can by hand.
Lower the car completely, then tighten the nuts.	Turn the wrench counterclockwise to lower the car, and then tighten the nuts with the wheel wrench. Tighten each nut a little at a time doing opposite ones until they are all tight.
Put the bad tire and tools back into the trunk.	Make sure you remove the blocks from under the tires before you drive away. Put the tire and tools away securely.

You can see that for a new trainee, the hints can make a big difference in learning. With pieces of equipment or processes, the hints may be referring to a special knob or key, a color that goes on, a sound you hear, a message you get on a screen, or mentioning a time delay. When you are doing a job breakdown, ask yourself, or anyone you're working with, about the *little details*, and be constantly thinking, "If I were new to this, what would help me learn?" Those are the things to include in the hints portion.

Checklist

Now that you have a *job breakdown* prepared, you may want to make it into a quick *checklist* as a reminder to the learner who no longer needs the hints portion of the job breakdown. That's easy; just use what is on the *steps* side of the job breakdown.

Checklist 1.1—How to Change a Flat Tire

	Pull the car off the road.
	Park the car.
	Get the spare tire, wrench, and jack out of the trunk.
	Loosen the wheel nuts before raising the car.
	Position the jack under the car.
	Jack the car up.
	Remove the wheel nuts and tire.
	Put the spare tire on.
	Put the wheel nuts back on.
	Lower the car completely and tighten the nuts.
	Put the bad tire and tools back into the trunk securely.

Performance Checks (PCs)

Performance Checks (PCs) are a trainers' tool used to determine if learning occurred, and, if not, what additional training is needed. We use this instead of a test. It is an evaluation of the trainee's ability, but it's taken from a more positive position. A *test* is usually a threatening word that creates anxiety. A PC is an aid to make sure that learning has occurred, or to help decide what additional assistance is needed from the trainer. In keeping with the procedure we started, we again use the same steps, from the job breakdown, in an easy-to-use format. It's a good idea to number each PC for ease in tracking.

Performance Check 2.1

Name of Trainee_____ Date_____

Performance Check—Changing a Flat Tire			
Steps	Level of Performance		
	1	2	3
Pull the car off the road. Park the car.			
Get the spare tire, wrench, and jack out of the trunk.			
Loosen the wheel nuts before raising the car.			
Position the jack under the car.			
Jack the car up.			
Remove the wheel nuts and tire.			
Put the spare tire on.			
Put the wheel nuts back on.			
Lower the car completely and tighten the nuts.			
Put the bad tire and tools back into the trunk securely.			

1 = Unable to perform this step
2 = Needs additional coaching on this step
3 = Can perform this step independently

Comments:

Signatures:
The following signatures indicate that this task has been performed accurately and independently, and no additional training is required.

_____ Trainer _____ Date

_____ Trainee _____ Date

_____ Supervisor _____ Date

Troubleshooting Guide

Troubleshooting guides are very important in both the initial learning and the ongoing operation and maintenance of your new process/equipment. Training is only half done without the troubleshooting portion, because, as we all know, things never seem to work exactly as the directions say when you are on your own. Sometimes the troubleshooting guide is the only tool you have to help you when things go wrong. This may be in the form of an expert system, a troubleshooting screen on your computer or MMI, or a handheld paper format. We'll demonstrate only the handheld paper format.

The easiest way to build a troubleshooting guide is in the three-stage format—what is the problem (that's what you're experiencing), what caused it, and how you fix it (possible solutions). Here's a sample, again using the flat tire example.

Troubleshooting Guide—Changing a Flat Tire

Problem	Possible Causes	Possible Solutions
Car is rolling.	• No blocks under tires.	• Find blocks and place in front of front tires and behind back tires.
	• Parked on uneven surface.	• Move car to level surface.
	• Emergency brake not on.	• Put emergency brake on.
Wheel nuts won't come loose.	• Too tight for you.	• Grab the wrench at the end to gain as much leverage as possible.
	• You're turning the wrench in the wrong direction.	• Turn in opposite direction.
Spare tire not secure.	• Corrosion on the mounting surface.	• Wipe off any corrosion from the mounting surface for good metal-to-metal contact.
	• Nuts not tight enough.	• Tighten nuts a little at a time, and in an opposite sequence, rather than all at once in a row.

Again, you can see that this is a simple-to-use format. It's best to start with the problem, because that's usually where you are when you need this guide. By building your own troubleshooting guides, you have the flexibility to update them continually. It's a great learning exercise to ask your trainees, once they have been doing the task/job a short time, to help you improve and/or update them.

LESSONS LEARNED

- Job Performance Aids are a *must have* in learning situations. Most vendors don't have them because the manual is the traditional tool. If that is the only learning tool they have available, look inside the manual, and I guarantee that you can easily take pieces out that can be made into JPAs. Most manuals do have troubleshooting guides that can be extracted for use without the manual.

- It's a wonderful learning exercise to have your people help you develop JPAs. It will reinforce their learning while building valuable tools for others. A company that I worked with had an extensive apprenticeship program. Once trainees became journeypeople, they had to develop new learning materials, and then teach using them. It was an excellent experience for all, and it kept their training materials, and them, fresh and current.

- I have found that a *great* place to find JPAs that people have made for themselves is to look in a craftsperson's toolbox. (You ask them first, of course.) They have wonderful drawings and quick-steps checklists. We did this, and once we cleaned them up a bit, we found them to be in high demand by others doing the same tasks.

- In a production environment, it's pretty important to laminate most JPAs since they are subject to dust, dirt, and heavy use. We often attached them to pieces of equipment by using light chains. This allowed easy access and helped to keep them from disappearing. It's no guarantee, but it's helpful.

- Let end users help you decide what JPAs are needed and then help to develop them. In this age of computerization, the use of tables and the ability to insert graphs and photos is easy and inexpensive. Investing in a digital camera is well worth the cost.

- Another way to decide when a JPA is needed is to look at the areas where the most problems occur.

- The samples shown can be used for independent JPAs or to develop an entire training program. This can be done internally with your current staff, or you could also use an intern or co-op to help you.
- Avoid using the word "test"—it's very threatening and creates unnecessary anxiety.

The concept of *Performance Checks* was a new one to each of the sites where I introduced it. If you are working with unions, it is *very important* that you spend adequate time explaining the tool and the process. You also need to administer it in the intention described. Union officials will immediately be skeptical and think that this is formal documentation that can be used against an employee. They may feel that it would violate seniority rules and be unfair. When developing this process, we learned that these are the safest and most useful guidelines to use.

Performance Check Guidelines:

- PCs are *informal* tools to evaluate whether learning has occurred and what additional training is needed. (*Not* to punish anyone.)
- The completed PC forms should be kept separate from trainees' formal personnel files, and not used as a tool to terminate an employee. It may disqualify trainees from a specific job (after sufficient training has occurred), but *not terminate* them.
- If internal hourly trainers are administering the PCs to the trainees, which is normal, a final performance check should be conducted by the supervisor or salaried training coordinator. Unions usually don't like their members to be evaluating other members, as the sole evaluators. We had the hourly trainers do the initial performance checks, and then when the trainee had completed all of their performance checks, the supervisor would conduct a final check. This is a good way for the supervisor to check on both the trainee and the trainer, to ensure that there is consistent use of the process. This is also a good way to identify what additional coaching the trainer may need.
- *Be consistent*—It's always the *golden rule!*
- Make sure that trainees understand what performance checks are and how and when they are being used.

By applying these guidelines consistently in all the locations I implemented this, an employee was never terminated due to the performance check process. In many labor-management discussions about performance checks, we were always allowed to continue their use because of our consistent and fair application.

Without an evaluation tool, you'll never know for sure
if learning has occurred!

APPRECIATIVE INQUIRY APPLICATION

Chapter 7—Documentation

In Chapter 7, We Discussed:

- The importance of knowing what kind of documentation you want and need, and then knowing how to ask your vendors for it.
- How to develop your own training and documentation specs.
- The value of Job Performance Aids (JPAs), and samples of some of the most common ones you can develop internally.
- The importance of partnership with your vendors—identifying everyone's expectations, as well as being flexible and realistic with one another.
- How to work effectively with unions when introducing performance checks.

From an *Appreciative Inquiry* point of view, no specific questions were listed in this section, but you can still apply it in your approach while developing specs and documentation. When working with vendors, you need to respect their capabilities and limitations. When developing documentation and training, find out what their *best* is. Ask them questions directly, like:

- Show me examples of some of the best training and documentation you have provided or seen. What made it good? (Best of *what is.*)
- If you don't have a good example but know what would make your documentation and/or training the *best*, what would it look like? (What *could be.*)

- What, from those examples, do you have the resources to provide? (What *will be*.)

- What support from us would you need to match or exceed those *best* experiences? (What *could be*.)

- Also ask yourself what your *best* is in these areas. For example, if you have excellent trainers, and (the vendors) have excellent materials, find a way to use the best of both. (What *could be*.) Perhaps this is by having your trainers work side by side with the designers/installers, using their materials. Then have your trainers do the training with one of their people available as backup to help when needed. (What *will be*.) No one is good at everything—be realistic and creative. Find the *best* of *what is* and open up new possibilities by creating what *could be* and *will be*! Solid partnerships make this happen. The synergy of the partnering, and the use of AI questions, opens up so many positive possibilities.

QUESTIONS TO ASK ABOUT DOCUMENTATION

Vendors

- What resources does your vendor have in the way of formal documentation and training?

- Who are the best contacts to talk to?

- Are there samples they can provide? References to contact?

- How much will it cost to have the vendor provide all the training and the documentation? Do we have the money to pay for it? How long will it take?

- Do we have a third party to recommend to them for training documentation?

- What platform do they develop their materials on?

- How flexible are they in altering their materials to meet your specs? How flexible are you in accepting what they have?

- How do they evaluate trainees? Measure learning?

- Are they open to training your trainers at their worksite and using your internal trainers as cotrainers?

- What resources/expectations do they have of you to support your project needs?

Internally

- Do we have specs in writing? If not, who could develop them? What do we want included?
- Who will coordinate the entire training documentation process?
- If you decide to develop training documentation internally, who is capable of that? How long will it take? What format will you use?
- How will the materials be validated?
- How will you ensure that materials are updated?
- Are there any grants available that could help pay for these materials?
- Are there any software packages for job aids?

8

Celebrate, Celebrate!
Rewards and Recognition

Everyone needs to feel appreciated—during a project this is especially true. Although project work can be very exciting and a wonderful professional growth opportunity, it can also be the root of much new stress. As was mentioned in the first few chapters of this book, project team members are often still doing their regular job, so this is all "extra" work. There are new deadlines to meet, new relationships to develop, and new processes/equipment that don't always work as promised. A project team needs to find ways to show encouragement, support and appreciation through rewards and recognition during the entire process—not just at the end!

Rewards and recognition during projects should happen:

- Now
- Then
- Whenever

Now means do it when something goes well—*don't wait*. Be specific about what you are appreciating, and do it as quickly after it happens as possible. *Then* means at the planned milestones, and *whenever* means just that—whenever there is a need to give the team or specific team members a "thank you." That could be after an unusually grueling day, after a particularly good day when you finally got something to work, or when an abrupt change has occurred, as they so often do. Keeping morale up is always a part of the people side of project management. The following pages will give you some examples of creative as well as traditional ways to say "thank you." Remember, it doesn't have to take a lot of time or cost a lot of money. In fact, usually the best approaches just require heart and a little time.

HOW REWARDING FOR PROJECTS IS DIFFERENT

Project teams are usually short term (six to nine months or less), so it's important to reward and recognize teamwork as well as individual performance. Be careful not to make all of the recognition individual, because you may create jealousies and alienation among the members, which will negatively influence the flow of the project and the end results. You'll notice that the examples on the following pages will emphasize fun (morale/team building) and group achievement. This doesn't mean people that go above and beyond shouldn't be recognized, but try to do it in a nonmaterialistic way so others can focus on the performance achieved by the team, not just by a person. They also emphasize the importance of old fashioned one-to-one acknowledgement and its value.

CAPITAL PROJECT HIERARCH OF NEEDS—REWARDS AND RECOGNITION

Although you've already seen this in Chapter 3, it's worth repeating here because it will help you look at your team, identify where they fall on the hierarchy of needs ladder, and what form of recognition may be most appropriate.

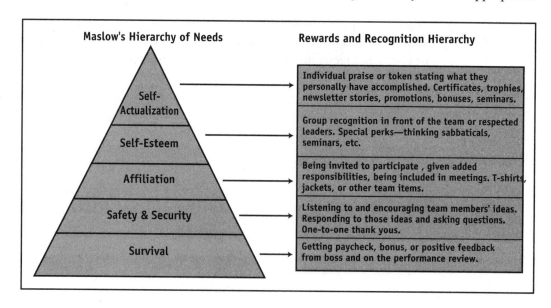

Corresponding Project Hierarchy of Needs

Self-Actualization	Team members want to feel that they individually have made a difference and have achieved their personal goals.
Self-Esteem	Team members want to feel good about their contributions, and the ability to utilize their skills. They want respect and recognition—being a part of a winning team.
Affiliation	Team members want to feel included and that they belong by being invited to meetings and kept updated with ongoing communications.
Safety and Security	Team members want to know that it's safe to freely contribution ideas freely, and that they can be open without fear of retribution.
Survival	Team members want to know that they will still be getting paychecks to pay their bills. They also need to know that they will still have jobs after the project is over, and that their project efforts will be recognized positively on their performance reviews.

REWARDS AND RECOGNITION BASICS

Be Timely—Give the recognition or reward as close as possible to the time the accomplishment happens.

Be Specific—Say or write exactly what performance you are rewarding and why (the positive results of the performance).

Be Sincere—Your words and actions must come from your heart, or it will be perceived suspiciously and not have the positive effect you are hoping for.

Private versus Public Praise—Caution

It's important that you be sensitive to the individual when giving rewards and recognition. Some people would rather crawl in a hole then have to stand up to receive an award or be praised publicly. When in doubt, you may just ask people if they have any objection to whatever public recognition you plan to give. Don't ruin a good thing by embarrassing a very shy or humble person.

SOMETHING OLD—TRADITIONAL REWARDS WITH A TWIST

Here are some of the traditional things that project teams do to reward and recognize team members for their efforts, but with a creative touch added.

- *The Infamous T-shirt*—Probably the most often-used token of appreciation is the team T-shirt. Everyone enjoys them, but usually they are selected from a catalog by one team member and not tied into performance. Here are a few twists to the traditional T-shirt recognition:

- *The Team-Designed T-shirt*—This is a great team-building activity in the beginning stages of your project. While the team is just forming, ask the members to describe the ideal team they want to be. Then ask them, in small groups, to draw and name it. Vote on the best one, and have that made into a team T-shirt. You'd be surprised at how much hidden creativity there is within any team. It'll be unique and begin to bond the team members.

- *The Piecemeal T-shirt*—For one project, we were always giving maintenance a hard time for not making the meetings. As an incentive, we told the managers that we'd give them a piece of a T-shirt every time they attended the meetings. If they attended all the meetings, we promised we'd sew the pieces together into a whole shirt. It became quite a fun focal point each week, and they never missed a meeting again. To make it interesting too, we numbered and drew on each piece. We added a word or two of praise on each piece. When they received the sewn-together shirt, the manager wore it with pride. It was then hung on his office for others to see. It was a conversation piece and a constant reminder of positive things they had done.

- *The Pizza Party Thank You*—

  - Rather than serving pizza, try a "make your own sundae" party for an after-lunch meeting. As they arrive, the team members can create their own ice cream treat—fun and inexpensive!

  - Rather than a real pizza, have a fake sliced pizza in a box, with each team member's name on top of one of the pieces. On the back side, write how that person contributes positively to the team, or mention the thing you like most about that person that spices up the project. Maybe even label them, "Jim is the 'sauce' because...," "Jane the 'meat' because..." etc.

Old Standbys, What Could Be Simplier—10 Minutes or Less

- *The handshake*—Look the person squarely in the eye, shake his or her hand, and say, "Thanks for... It really made a difference by..." Always mention *specifically what the person did*, and *what the results were*. This is about the oldest form of appreciation, and it's still as effective as it always was. Depending on the person, doing it in front of a group may add to the value of it.

- *The email*—In this day and age, email can be a real blessing, especially when you only have a minute and you don't want to forget to say "thanks" to someone. It's quick, it's easy, and the people receiving it can see your words in writing, perhaps even copy them as a reminder of their accomplishments. Don't forget that a "thanks" in person is best, but this is much better than forgetting. You can follow up your email with a call or visit, to reinforce your appreciation. Sometimes, adding a clip art picture adds a nice touch!

- *The e-Flash*—This is another form of email thanks, but it goes out to the total project team or even a larger group list. In a survey I recently did on generational diversity, it was interesting to note that all age groups wanted more appreciation, and most groups wanted it in front of others. This helps to meet people's need for acceptance and self-esteem on the hierarchy of needs.

- *The give that person a cigar award*—On a large piece of paper, symbolizing a cigar, simply write down what the person did in big letters. Award them to people at team meetings. Once, at the end of my son's little league season, the coach gave all of the children two of these paper awards, one for the thing they did best, and one for the thing they most improved on. These often were quite comical and creative. They were received with such pride, and they were merely handwritten on legal-size paper. A key too was that everyone got two, so they all felt important.

- *The post-it note recognition*—Have a *project board* where any project announcements get posted. Have a pad of post-it notes attached so that anyone can write a good word or two about the project or any team member and post it there for everyone to see.

- *The brewing phone call*—This again is an easy and non-time-consuming way to say "thanks." Once again, from my survey, people wanted a personal interaction more than anything else when getting recognized. With the call invite the person for a cup of coffee and 10 uninterrupted minutes of your time and attention.

Always share these words of praise with the project members' managers!

The Traditional Bag of Recognition Goodies

Included in this bag might be: gift certificates, hats, mugs, duffle bags, shirts, jackets, T-shirts, pens, trophies, certificates of appreciation, pens, ESOPs, bonuses, promotions, educational opportunities, lunch, dinner, story and/or picture in the company newsletter.

SOMETHING NEW—60 MINUTES OR LESS

- *The "round robin" appreciation*—This may be one of those "then" forms of appreciation that you do after reaching some project milestone, or at the end. Each person has a piece of $8^1/_2 \times 11$ paper, and puts his or her name on the top, which he or she then passes to the next person. That person then writes down how the person whose name is on top of the paper has contributed to the team/project. Each paper gets passed around so that each team member has written a few positive words about all the other team members. The team leader or facilitator then reads each one out loud and hands the paper to the person it belongs to. As many times as I have done this, it has always brought goodwill and a sense of accomplishment to all involved. Many people keep them in their wallets for those days when they need to hear something good about themselves. It's important that everyone gets praise rather than just a few people, especially during projects.

- *The silly subject awards*—Pick several fun categories and find associated awards to go along with them. For example, the "golden broom" or "golden hammer" award might go to the one who made the biggest physical or housekeeping improvement during the week. Or the "golden alarm" award could go to the person who "saved the day" from an alarming situation. Spray painting a hammer, broom, or alarm golden is inexpensive. Passing it around weekly, to new people or departments, brings laughter while you're saying thanks.

- *Coins in the pocket recognition*—At the beginning of the day, put five coins in your right pocket. During the day, make it a point to say something positive to someone. Each time you do, take a coin out of the right pocket and put it into the left pocket. At the end of the day if all the coins have moved, you'll know you recognized at least five people. You can create many different versions of this.

- *Capturing the best of* what is *in a "Best Practices" journal*—At each meeting, or whenever, ask for examples of things that went well. Capture those in writing and build a journal, adding pictures whenever possible. You could even build a Project Book out of it and hand it out at the project's completion, as recognition and a learning tool that they could all have to remember the project and the lessons learned from it. Have a recorder at each meeting, or just ask people to jot these things down and give them to a designated person who will log them. You may also think about having an information manager for the project that does this. Too often, all those little things along the way get forgotten, or there no longer is time to review them at the end when people are getting reassigned to new projects. You might even add this portion to the project *shared folder* on the computer so it could be done at any time, day or night, without the need for a recorder.

- *The fortune cookie rewards*—At the project meetings have special project fortune cookies to give out freely to anyone who notably contributes with a good idea, comment, question, etc. To make these, just buy some fortune cookies, take the fortunes out with tweezers, then replace them with ones you've made. It's really quite easy. The comments on them should reflect typical words of praise that would be offered during your project. For example, "The person who offers new ideas often saves the project," or "Asking the right questions saves time and money," or just plain "Great job—we're glad you are on the team." Give them out freely to as many people as appropriate.

- *The project big shot*—This celebrates someone who has gone above and beyond on the project. On a flip-chart piece of paper (or maybe two taped together), draw a body outline representing that person. Have all the team members add their artistic, or not, talents to it by drawing or writing in what makes that person so special. (Do this prior to the meeting.) Write comments all over the body outline, mentioning little and big things that person has contributed to the success of the project. At the next meeting, have it covered, and let it be the last bullet on the meeting agenda. Then have fun introducing, unveiling, and sharing what it says to the team and the honored team member. (Obliviously, this isn't something to do to someone who would hate getting all this public attention.) Another approach is to have a "big shot" of the month to give everyone a chance at the spotlight.

- *Have a breakfast of champions*—Have this for people who have supported the project team—they often do a lot of work with little acknowledgement. Invite them to the breakfast, then while they are eating, say and hand each person a word of appreciation for what they have done. Again, *make this specific*. We used this as a plantwide program. Anyone could nominate anyone else. Those selected monthly then were invited to a breakfast with the plant manager. They received certificates of appreciation, but they also had an open forum to ask the plant manager anything they wanted to know about the business. This was very inexpensive, and very effective. Having audience with the "top person" was what they valued the most. Once, a new manager came in and "beefed up" the rewards by adding jackets to our previous prizes of just certificates and donuts. It then became competitive, union complaints surfaced, and it eventually was discontinued. So the lesson is KISS—keep it simple, stupid!

SOMETHING BORROWED...

The best way to learn is by watching or listening to what others have done that worked. The following are a few examples of unique ways to reward and recognize others for jobs well done, taken from *CARE Packages for the Workplace* and *Handle with CARE—Motivating and Retaining Your Employees,* written by Barbara A. Glanz.

WOW—Within Our Walls

This is a program at Lands' End for employees to recognize the positive things that other employees do at any level. They fill out a WOW form for the recognition, the people get their pictures posted with the recognition, and at the end of the month, a drawing is held for a small gift.

Within Our Walls Award

To: _____Date:_____
From: _____, your friend in Reedsburg.
I think you're great!
You really made a difference because ...

"Pass It Along" Cards

Barbara Glanz, an international speaker and author, uses these as her personal signature whenever she speaks to a group. Each person is given a "PASS IT

ALONG" card that says, "Some people make the world a more special place just by being in it." On the back it says, "PASS IT ALONG." She encourages everyone to pass it along within 48 hours to someone else who has done some little thing to make a difference in their lives. They come with many different sayings. Some companies have created their own cards with the appropriate wording for their work environments. You can easily put them on someone's desk, in a drawer, or anywhere that the person will find them.

"I'm Going to Tell Your Mother" Recognition

A manager was down in the dumps because, once again, his work team came out lowest on the productivity chart. Out of frustration, he challenged his crew by saying, "If we can improve and win the productivity award, I promise I'll call each of your mothers and tell them what a good employee you are." The crew of rather senior employees laughed it off and said, "Sure you will." He sincerely reiterated his promise several times, so the crew played along to see if he'd be true to his word. Yes, you guessed it. They beat all the other teams, won the award, and the manager called each and every mom. The surprised mothers were shocked to be getting a call about their adult children but were so pleased. When the mothers called their sons and daughters to share the call they got, the moms were beaming with pride...and, of course, the crew members' self-esteem was bolstered tremendously.

And here's another idea, this one borrowed from Alexander Hiam's *Motivating and Rewarding Employees.*

- A "thinking sabbatical" is a day away from the project and any other normal duties to do some thinking about ways to improve performance on the project. The person can be given a special "thinking" pen and pad of paper, and just be given the time to write down or sketch new ideas. The next day, the person then presents the new ideas to the appropriate people. This would be most appropriate for the person who is always coming up with new ideas *or could* if the time were available. It might also be used as an incentive for others, showing that ingenuity and accomplishment is being rewarded.

Rewards and recognition should always bring a sense of pride and satisfaction, or so we thought. While building the first team-based line at a large facility, we went out of our way to train the team members thoroughly and give them every learning opportunity possible. They were often treated to trips out of town to visit other locations that we could learn from and emulate, special lunches, meetings, and T-shirts. It didn't take long before the others in the facility grew tired of their special treatment and began to alienate them. At first, this seemed a bit like sour grapes since everyone had the opportunity initially to go through the selection process. But once it got to the point that people refused to help out the team because "they didn't have the training," it grew to be a bottom-line problem. We learned our lesson, and from then on took greater care in how we rewarded people on projects.

Another experience, at a different facility, that helped avoid the alienation problem was to have some special opportunities going on for many and/or all people at the same time. Again, we were introducing the first team-based line with a formal selection process, but we also introduced a crafts skill upgrade program, literacy classes, tuition reimbursement, and a train-the-trainer program for all classifications. Because nearly everyone in the plant had some opportunity made available to them, no one felt that anyone else was getting special treatment. We never once had to deal with the alienation issue.

LESSONS LEARNED

- Rewards and recognition should be tied to *performance*; otherwise they are meaningless. Performance can mean many things—improvement, reaching a goal, helping other people reach their goal, etc. You can't always measure it in definite numbers, but you should be able to articulate specifically what it is, and what the result of the team or person's action was.

- Behavior that is rewarded gets repeated!

- Rewards and recognition, during projects, should focus on team accomplishments first, then individual ones. These people have to work together to reach the goals, and if only a few get praise, it may cause a lot of friction within the project team.

- The small, personal appreciative words and gestures go a long way during projects. They should be given out generously to keep morale up and build relationships while you are reinforcing good performance. The team's life span is short, so you need to remember to show appreciation whenever it's warranted. Make it fun and easy to give and receive.

- Alienation is a problem when it comes to project recognition—think not only about what you are doing for the team, but how it will affect others. This is especially true when the rewards are tangible, like dinners, T-shirts, hats, duffle bags, etc. This doesn't mean that you can't or shouldn't do them, but it should make you see how the personal appreciative interactions can all around be more effective.

- In most surveys on what people want, the ratings usually favor personal thanks and/or public recognition over any other item. Spending quality time with a person, and growth opportunities, are also high on people's lists. Of course, most people think that money is first, but the late May Kay Ash, CEO of Mary Kay Cosmetics, sums it up nicely when she said, "There are two things people want more than money and sex—recognition and praise."

- Don't praise someone and then follow that with the infamous "but." The old "one-two" does a lot of damage that is hard to recover from. Reward and recognize good performance separately from coaching and counseling poor performance. Never tie them in together!

- Don't be afraid to ask people what form of appreciation and recognition they most value.

APPRECIATIVE INQUIRY APPLICATION

Section 8—Rewards and Recognition

In Chapter 8, We Discussed:
- The importance of ongoing appreciation to a project team and its members
- When and how to reward and recognize project teams
- Examples of quick and easy approaches
- Things to be careful of when recognizing project teams

When thinking about Appreciative Inquiry, we are always inquiring about the best of *what is* as the base for what *could be* and *will be*. One of the best examples mentioned is *the best of "what is" journal*, which could evolve into a Best Practices booklet. By capturing these examples throughout the project, you are continually reinforcing the assets of the team and its members. It then becomes a tool to create what *could* and *will be* in the future, completing the Appreciative Inquiry Process. The trick is to make this easy to manage and do. The project manager should encourage this at the project meetings by always starting with, "tell me about the things that went well," and using those examples as springboards for new possibilities for what *could* and *will be*. By using the "shared folder" approach, these "best ofs" can be collected and referred back to at any time. When people hear, then see the positive, it's rewarding to them, but it also builds an optimistic picture for future possibilities. Remember that these need to be fact based and sincere in order to be meaningful.

Another example of AI questions is

- At that kickoff meeting, you could even have a fun card that asks the following questions (see Chapter 3).

  Thinking back to your past experiences, what have been the most meaningful ways that you or your team was recognized? (Best of what is.)

- What forms of recognition would you *personally like to be thanked for a job well done?* How does that motivate you?

- What motivates you to do your best? Describe an example of that.

Use these *best of* answers to develop what *could* and *will be*.

QUESTIONS TO ASK ABOUT REWARDS AND RECOGNITION

- When starting a project, ask how you will show appreciation for team and individual accomplishments.
- Is there any money in your budget for any special rewards, if you plan any?
- What project milestones would be good for special recognition?

Final Thoughts

After the many pages of ideas and sample forms, I keep hoping that the survey participants, and the many others they represent, will see the relationship between their concerns and what's been said in the *Project Management Workbook*. Because of that, I felt the need to finish my book with these final thoughts that will help to put the pieces together.

Survey Participants' Concerns

Some of the greatest "people" concerns expressed about project work revolved around:

- How to comanage a project and deal with turf battles
- Lack of and insufficient communication
- How to deal with conflicting priorities and lack of commitment
- How to train people for new technology
- Individual and hidden agendas
- How to develop and motivate a team
- Dealing with uncooperative team members, sabotage, and politics

I won't try to answer all of these concerns in any depth since I've chosen not to do a behavioral theory book. What I will do is offer guidelines, and references to appropriate chapters, that can get you started in the right direction. The following can be utilized by any project manager or participant.

AS A PROJECT MANAGER OR PARTICIPANT

- Understand people's project needs (Chapters 1, 2, 3, and 8)—Refer to the hierarchy of needs in Chapter 3, and use that information wisely. A little effort goes a long way. Think of what problem you're experiencing with some of the team members, and see where they fall in the spectrum of needs.

- Build a team and many partnerships (Chapters 2, 3, and 8)—Going back to *needs* is key to enhancing the working relationships and eliminating many project *issues*.
  - Take the time at the beginning to identify expectations, write them down, and decide how you will resolve issues before they happen.
  - Get people involved and empowered with information.
  - Find the best of what they have to offer and use it.
- Develop Partnership Agreements with vendors. (See Appendix.)
  This is time well spent and will pay the project back many times over. It's the old "we never plan enough" syndrome that kills many projects—add people issues to your planning. Being clear about expectations is an effective step not to be dismissed. Set clear objectives and follow up on them. COMMUNICATE, COMMUNICATE, AND COMMUNICATE! Any stakeholder in a project is never too small to be communicated with. Knowledge is empowering.
- Use the Appreciative Inquiry approach (Chapter 1, each chapter's "Appreciative Inquiry Application" portion, and the overview in the appendix)—Work from the *best* of what is, not from a "this is a problem to be solved" attitude.
- Reward and recognize (Chapters 3 and 8) generously, factually, sincerely, and frequently! As the old saying goes, "You can catch more bees with honey than vinegar." This is worth remembering and applying.
- Catch their spirit and energy (Chapters 2, 3, and 8) for the project as well as their individual successes. When people feel important and appreciated, they are much more productive. Make it fun to be a part of the team, even when the going is tough. Stress and crisis can fracture or bond a team—use them instead to build and strengthen yours. Think of how the tragedies of 9/11 brought the country and families together. Use your project crises wisely; they can demonstrate how anything is possible when you work together.
- Make training a priority (Chapters 2, 5, 6, and 7)—Stop assuming that it'll be done correctly, and create the groundwork for effective training and documentation at the start.

Final Reinforcing Thoughts

If I could reemphasize only one thing as being the most important of all, it would be the partnership concept. People working together, especially those who normally aren't in leadership positions, make things happen and usually surpass your expectations. Don't forget always to include the end users. My experience is that the nonmanagerial people are the most *untapped* resource in most industries today! They are just waiting to share their thoughts and ideas, but *only* if they know that you are sincere about listening and doing something with those ideas.

> Never doubt that a small group
> Of thoughtful, committed people
> can change the world.
> Indeed, it is the only thing that ever has.
> —Margaret Mead

Appendix: Appreciative Inquiry and Partnership Agreement

Appreciative Inquiry is a method of discovering, understanding, and fostering innovations in organizations through the gathering of positive stories and images and the construction of positive interactions. It seeks out the very best of *what is* in order to help ignite the collective imagination of *what could be*. The aim is to generate new knowledge that expands the realm of the possible and helps members of an organization envision a collectively desired future and to carry forth that vision in ways that successfully translate images of possibility into reality, and beliefs into practice.

Appreciative Inquiry can be a helpful tool in any planning effort that requires strategic vision and an empowering context for innovation and development.

Here is a brief summary of the process and principles behind it:

Appreciation:

1. *You discover the best of what is*, and value those factors that give life to the organization; for example, what do you value most about yourself, your coworkers, and the organizations of which you are a part? What, in your view, is making a positive difference in the quality of life in your organization? What contributions are you making that you are especially proud of?

2. *You envision what could be.* When the best of what is has been identified and is valued, the mind begins to search beyond, to imagine new possibilities. Imagining involves passionate thinking, allowing yourself to be inspired by what you see. It means creating a positive image of a desired future, e.g., what small initiative/project would make a big difference in your work area?

3. *You engage in dialogue*, discussing and sharing discoveries and possibilities. Through dialogue, individual vision becomes shared vision.

4. *You create the future of what will be through innovation and action.* Because ideals are grounded in realities, there is confidence to make things happen.

Inquiry:

1. *Inquiry into what is possible should begin with appreciation.* The primary task is to describe and explain those exceptional moments that give energy to the organization/project and activate members' competencies and energies.

2. *Inquiry into what's possible should be applicable.* Study should lead to the creation of knowledge that can be used, applied, and validated in action.

3. *Inquiry into what is possible should be provocative.* An organization is capable of becoming more than it is at any given moment, and of learning how to determine its own future.

4. *Inquiry into the human potential in the organization should be collaborative.* This assumes an inseparable relationship between the process of inquiry and its content.

SIX ASPECTS OF CHANGE AND DEVELOPMENT OF WHICH TO BE AWARE:

1. *Knowledge of the organization is critical to determining its destiny.* To be effective change agents, we must understand organizations as living constructions. Understanding the organization is at the center of any movement towards positive change. Thus, the way we know is fateful.

2. *The seeds of change are implicit in the first questions we ask.* The questions we ask determine what we find, and what we find becomes the material from which the future is conceived and change is made.

3. *A critical resource we have for creating positive change in the organization is our imagination,* and our capacity to free the imagination and mind of groups.

4. *Our imagination and mind are constrained by our bad habits,* limited styles of thinking, underlying assumptions, and traditional rules of organizing.

5. *Our styles of thinking rarely match the increasingly complex worlds in which we work*...therefore, we need to commit ourselves to the ongoing discovery of more creative and fruitful ways of knowing.

6. *Organizations,* as living constructions, are largely affirmative, and *respond to positive thought and positive knowledge.*

Two Contrasting Models of Planning

Problem Solving	**Appreciative Inquiry**

"Felt Need"
Identification of Problem

Appreciating and
Valuing the Best of What Is

Analysis of Causes

Envisioning What Could Be

Analysis of
Possible Solutions

Dialoguing about
What Should Be

Action Planning
(Treatment)

Innovating
What Will Be

Basic Assumption:
Organizing is a
Problem to be Solved

Basic Assumption:
Organizing is a
Mystery to be Embraced

See Cooperrider and Srivastva (1987) "Appreciative Inquiry Into Organizational
Life" in *Research in Organizational Change and Development*, Pasmore and Woodman
(eds), Vol. 1, JAI Press.

SOME EXAMPLES OF APPRECIATIVE INQUIRY QUESTIONS FOR USE IN A PROJECT SETTING

- What do you value most about yourself as a project team member?
  About the project of which you are a part?

- Describe a positive change that you've been involved with, possibly in your work area. How could you apply that to this project?
- What made it possible?
- What was something you learned about making change during projects?
- Describe one thing you would like to learn during this project and something you could teach others.
- What small change in your area might make a big difference?

Discovering Personal Interest in the Project: Three Positive Questions

1. Tell of a project experience that was a personal high point—an experience where you said to yourself, "People really can make a difference. I'm glad I got involved."
2. Why did this project experience mean so much to you?
3. If you were asked for three good reasons to get involved in the project, what would you say?

Guidelines for Good Questions:

- *State the question in a positive way.* E.g., What is something that you value about your workplace/project?
- *Ask for what you hope for, not what you're afraid of.* E.g., What would you like to do for the project (instead of what problems are you concerned about)?
- *Ask open-ended questions that encourage storytelling.*
- *Credit people for their positive qualities.* E.g., What is the best thing you have done for someone else this week? During a past project?
- *Help people remember project experiences that are worth appreciating and valuing.*
- *Get at people's most important, most meaningful concerns.* E.g., What was a high point, a project experience that was especially meaningful to you as an employee? Why did that mean so much?

Using the Above Guidelines, Design a Question That:

a) Helps you discover what your project team members care about
b) Identifies positive things happening in the project
c) Finds out about projects or work tasks that your employees like to do

SO HOW CAN THIS APPLY TO US?

Whatever your planning situation (project or otherwise) or need is, it can be addressed using this asset-based methodology called Appreciative Inquiry (AI), as opposed to a more negative, "what's wrong" approach. All studies show that your potential for achievement is exponentially higher when you begin from the positive. Your people truly can be your greatest asset if they are empowered by being allowed to utilize the skills, knowledge, and imagination they hold within them. AI is a way to get that out through this open dialogue approach.

Here are some of the Frequently Asked Questions (FAQs): You may have more.

- *So what happens to the "problems" if you are using AI instead of typical problem-solving techniques?* The problems are addressed, but from a new, more innovative perspective. For example, rather than talking about the safety "problems" in the workplace, you can talk about areas that *are* safe in the workplace and why, what makes them safe, and what practices you already have that are working. The stories and experiences from there can then bring forth ideas about how to create a safer workplace. The action plans evolve from there to resolve the problems. You have identified your "best practices" and expanded upon them to apply to your current situation/project.

- *Do you have to have special training to facilitate AI?* The beauty of AI is that with some basic training and coaching, most anyone can do it. It's really about creating an environment where people can tell their positive stories. The best facilitator of the process is someone who is a good listener, is able to ask good, appreciative questions, and has a positive attitude about change and continuous improvement. This could be anyone, from the floor sweeper to the CEO. The concepts are really very simple.

When Bliss Browne was starting her organization, IMAGINE CHICAGO, high-school students were taught the AI questioning process. They then interviewed over 350 people, of all ranks and positions throughout the city, asking "What made Chicago a great city?" From the answers they created endless new possibilities, which then turned into exceptional programs that have contributed to innovative improvements in the city, especially with its educational programs. The ideas all came from finding the best of *what is*. Their successes have become the blueprint for giving cities and organizations around the world new hope for creating desired futures. You can do the same in your organization and with your project. Checkout www.imaginechicago.org.

- *If it's so good, how come I've never heard of it?* It's actually a fairly new methodology (within the last 10 years) that David Cooperrider developed at Case Western University. It's a component of the Organizational Development field that is now being introduced into many management programs. Its applications and successes have been demonstrated worldwide in all types of organizations.

- *Why is AI so good during change?* People are usually fearful of the unknown—that's what change is about. They feel uncertain about whether they can adjust to the change—it's all very foreign and frightening. They don't want to look stupid or lose what they are comfortable with. AI begins with the best of their *known* environment and moves forward toward new provocative possibilities, carrying along the positive experiences of what has already worked well. They become a part of designing the change process, creating a synergistic environment. Self-esteem is enhanced. *They take the* best of what is, *imagine* what could be *and create what* will be!

- *How does this apply to project work?* Projects are usually vehicles of change, which as we already mentioned creates fear in many. A.I. helps to reduce or eliminate that fear fear by holding onto the good from the past, and funnel that energy in a more positive direction by bringing people into the planning and designing process. Since projects are usually short term, they need to move forward as quickly and effectively as possible. By identifying the best of *what is* you can accelerate the project's progress by utilizing the now-known capabilities within your team members. Check out the Appreciative Inquiry Web site for more information (www.appreciativeinquiry.cwru.edu).

BUILDING A PARTNERSHIP AGREEMENT: VENDOR AND COMPANY AS TRAINING PARTNERS

Companies and Their Vendors Have the Same Goal: Efficient, Reliable Equipment/Process/Systems

Aside from the technical functioning of the new equipment/process/system, effective training is one of the most significant ways to ensure high efficiencies for your project. When equipment/processes/systems are down, costs mount up exponentially. To support your project's new installation sufficiently, representatives from the equipment/process/system manufacturer and the company should sit down and discuss their training expectations of one another, along with their training goals. Here are some of the issues that may need to be discussed:

Some of the constant barriers to good training are:

- Insufficient time, changing schedules
- The wrong people in training
- Distractions—noise, phones, poor training facilities
- Trainees being pulled from class
- Not being able to train on the equipment
- Too many trainees in class
- Poor or no documentation
- Poor communication (internally and externally) about class schedules, participants assigned, overtime arrangements
- Poor or no record keeping

These are just a few barriers. On the next page is a template that can easily be used to build a success agreement that will save valuable time and ensure higher levels of participation and shared responsibility for learning.

Training Partnership Agreement

This TRAINING PARTNERSHIP AGREEMENT is between _____ (vendor) and _____ (company) for the success of project

_____.

The purpose of this agreement is to:

- Clarify our expectations of one another (yours, mine, ours)
- Decide how we will resolve issues related to this partnership
- Set mutual and measurable goals

Company expectations:
Vendor expectations:

Together we will collaborate and be accountable for:
In the event that confusion arises over the above we will resolve it by:
Specific and measurable training goals we will commit to:

Together we have discussed and agreed to this Partnership Agreement with the purpose of attaining the mutually identified training goals that support the success of the project.

_____Company Representative

_____ Vendor Representative

_____ Date

Training Partnership Agreement—Sample

This TRAINING PARTNERSHIP AGREEMENT is between Sydney Packing Manufacturer (vendor) and Sally Soda Bottler (company) for the success of project to install 4 XYZ packing machines.

The purpose of this agreement is to:

- Clarify our expectations of one another (yours, mine, ours.)
- Decide how we will resolve issues related to this partnership.
- Set mutual and measurable goals.

Company expectations: (from the vendor)

- A training proposal by (date)
- Training outlines, manuals and Job Aids to be reviewed by (date) (Details will be discussed further on the content)
- A training schedule to support our start-up timeline
- Qualified trainers
- Performance checks to measure individual learning
- A training contact to coordinate all training activities
- Trainers dedicated to training (not trying to install at the same time)

Vendor Expectations: (of the customer)

- A designated training contact/coordinator
- Appropriate trainees dedicated to training
- Sufficient dedicated time to train
- Training resources (as designated)
- Internal trainers support (if they are available, details to be discussed)
- Logistical coordination (room, online time, materials)
- Elimination of distractions, like pulling people from class (as best as can be expected)
- Preplanned schedule (a copy prior to arrival), sufficient notice of training requirement (i.e., training windows)
- Participants Profile and Needs Assessment forms completion
- Follow-up training/reinforcement plan
- Employee and union issues resolution

Together we will collaborate and be accountable for:

- Training schedule
- Follow-up training plan
- Assessment of trainees learning
- Record keeping for records and OSHA requirements
- Assessment of training needs
- Training content and tools
- Co-training, when appropriate

In the event that confusion arises over the above, we will resolve it by:

- Bringing up the specific issue as quickly as possible to the identified training contact and arrange to meet/discuss solution ASAP
- Bring solutions to the meeting—not blame
- Keep project goals as the prerequisite for solutions

Specific and measurable training goals we will commit to:

- Allow two internal trainers to train at Sydney Manufacturer's location for designated time. Those trainers will then assist with on-site training and follow-up plan

- Complete first round of training by (date)
- Do performance checks on each participant to identify what additional training is needed
- Develop a follow-up plan to reinforce learning

Together we have discussed and agreed to this Partnership Agreement with the sole purpose of attaining mutually identified training goals that support the success of the project.

_____ Company Representative

_____ Vendor Representative

_____ Date

Index

Note: **Boldface** numbers indicate illustrations.

ABOUT THE AUTHOR

Nancy Cobb, MS, MOB, is founder and president of the consulting firm PARTNERS in POSSIBILITIES, Inc. a firm specializing in Organizational Development interventions. Some of the main initiatives the firm works on in the Organizational Development arena are Needs Assessment , Change Management; Training— design, development and implementation; Project Management; Generational Diversity, Appreciative Inquiry, Business Alignment, and Performance Management (recruitment, retention, and recognition). Her consulting experience has been within manufacturing, nonprofit, service, and educational arenas. She also is a public speaker.

Nancy earned her B.A. in Education at Western Illinois University and her Master's of Organizational Behavior from Benedictine University, with her area of concentration in Organizational Development. After her undergraduate degree she was a teacher and social worker for several years. While in Boston she founded a nonprofit organization that set up internships for nontraditional students (adults), before moving into industry. She continued to be involved in education throughout her career; serving on professional organization's training task forces and Advisory Boards, at the college level, that focused on the collaboration of education and industry. She also was very active on literacy initiatives at the state and national level, serving on the President's Literacy Definition Committee in Washington, D.C. and the State of Illinois Literacy Advisory Board. She set up literacy programs at the industrial sites she worked at and spoke nationwide on the topic. She is also on the board of Imagine Chicago, a nonprofit organization that creates hopeful futures for people and organizations through the asset-based, appreciative inquiry approach to change.

She spent most of her career in manufacturing with Nabisco, at three different locations, always in the recruitment and organizational development area. She was a part of all the major change initiatives such as Socio-Technical Systems, Reengineering, Self-Directed Work Teams, Pay for Skills and Knowledge, Apprenticeship Programs and all major capital project teams, where she designed and integrated the cultural and technical changes. She designs and delivers her own materials and always emphasizes business alignment using a partnership approach, as well as the asset-based Appreciative Inquiry process.

ABOUT THE AUTHOR